# CONVERSATION SKILLS 2.0 AND RELATIONSHIP COMMUNICATION
# 2-in-1 Book

*The #1 Beginner's Guide to Improve Your Communication and Resolve Any Conflict in Just 7 days*

# CONVERSATION SKILLS 2.0 *TALK TO ANYONE AND DEVELOP MAGNETIC CHARISMA*

*Discover Cutting-Edge Methods to Enhance Your Communication Skills in Just 7 Days, Even If You're Shy or Introverted*

© Copyright 2019 by _____ - All rights reserved.

The following book is reproduced below with the goal of providing information that is as accurate and reliable as possible. Regardless, purchasing this book can be seen as consent to the fact that both the publisher and the author of this book are in no way experts on the topics discussed within and that any recommendations or suggestions that are made herein are for entertainment purposes only. Professionals should be consulted as needed prior to undertaking any of the action endorsed herein.

This declaration is deemed fair and valid by both the American Bar Association and the Committee of Publishers Association and is legally binding throughout the United States.

Furthermore, the transmission, duplication, or reproduction of any of the following work including specific information will be considered an illegal act irrespective of if it is done electronically or in print. This extends to creating a secondary or tertiary copy of the work or a recorded copy and is only allowed with the express written consent from the Publisher. All additional rights reserved.

The information in the following pages is broadly considered a truthful and accurate account of facts and as such, any inattention, use, or misuse of the information in question by the reader will render any resulting actions solely under their purview. There are no scenarios in which the publisher or the original author of this work can be in any fashion deemed liable for any hardship or damages that may befall them after undertaking information described herein.

Additionally, the information in the following pages is intended only for informational purposes and should thus be thought of as universal. As befitting its nature, it is presented without assurance regarding its prolonged validity or interim quality. Trademarks that are mentioned are done without written consent and can in no way be considered an endorsement from the trademark holder.

Conversation Skills
# Table of Contents

**Introduction** .................................................................................. 9

**Chapter 1 - Establishing Likability** ............................................. 13

    The Confirmation Bias .................................................................. 13

    The Qualities & Behaviors that Make You Instantly Likable ....... 15

    What Determines Likable Behavior? ............................................ 18

    The Seven Bad Habits that are Making You Unlikable ................ 20

**Chapter 2 - The Basics of Good Conversation** ........................... 24

    How to Make Great First Impressions .......................................... 24

    Win at Small Talk with the ARE Model ...................................... 29

    Three Essential Ways to Get Along with Anyone You Meet ....... 30

    Six Tips for Resisting Shyness and a Lack of Confidence ............ 34

**Chapter 3 - Igniting Exceptional Interactions** ............................ 39

    Conversation Topics & Tips for Every Possible Scenario ............ 39

    The Worst Mistakes You Can Make in a Conversation ................ 45

    Ideas to Steer Clear of Boring Conversations ............................... 51

    Three General Rules for Sparking an Interesting Conversation .... 53

**Chapter 4 - Cultivating Charisma and Magnetism** ..................... 56

    The Thirteen Secrets to Developing a Magnetic Personality ........ 57

    All You Need to Know About the Trifecta of Charm ................... 64

    Three Steps to Becoming a More Interesting Person .................... 72

**Chapter 5 - Knowing Your Audience** .......................................... 75

    Microexpressions ........................................................................... 75

    The Six Types of Communicators & How to Win Them Over ..... 79

    Conversation Tips for Special Audiences ..................................... 84

## Chapter 6 - Building Deep Connections .................................................. 87
Conversation Tricks to Instantly Build Rapport with Someone ... 88
How to Form Meaningful Relationships ....................................... 90
The Habits of Emotionally Intelligent People ............................... 93
Why Self-Compassion is Important for Healthy Relationships.... 96

## Chapter 7 - Difficult Situations & Social Blunders ...................... 99
How to talk your way out of difficult or awkward situations ....... 99
Coping with Difficult Personalities ............................................. 105
When is it okay to lie? ................................................................ 112

## Chapter 8 - Using Conversation to Get What You Want ......... 113
Subtle ways of showing dominance ............................................ 113
Persuasion Techniques for all Situations .................................... 115
Three Tricks to Seduce Someone through Conversation ............ 118
Six Highly Effective Tips for Successful Negotiations ............... 121

## Conclusion .................................................................................... 124

Conversation Skills
# **Introduction**

I know the real reason you opened this book: you're desperate to see change in your day-to-day life. You're bored of lackluster social interactions, a dead-end career and you're disappointed by your strained or unfulfilling relationships. You know it can get better - you've seen other people develop the kind of relationships you desire - and you want to own that kind of social influence now.

This may surprise you, but you're not the only one who feels this way. Leagues of people across the world dream of these same changes and, like you, they have a hunch that the solution lies in amping-up their social abilities. Like you, they want to be a conversational master.

But the good news is, you're already one step ahead of them.

Why? It's simple. You've taken the first step. You've opened this book. You're about to commit to greater achievements and more powerful relationships – and that makes you a tad smarter than the rest. Congratulations on getting a little closer to your goals.

Perhaps you're awkward and shy. Perhaps, you constantly feel overpowered in social settings, like your presence doesn't matter. You never know the right thing to say and it feels like you're always one beat behind the rest.

Or perhaps, you're not socially awkward at all, you simply want to wield more influence over your peers and make a stronger impact on everyone you meet. You've seen the way some people get what they want using only their words, and you want to experience what it's like. I'll tell you now, this experience can be yours with some practice and expert wisdom. It's not as difficult as it looks, you just need the right training.

Whatever stage you're at, whether you're a timid wallflower or a fairly confident conversationalist, this book will take you to the same destination: the top of your communication game. This book will show you the entire spectrum, from the very basics of good conversation to the advanced tools of persuasion and influence. We'll break down language, behavior, and personality into their digestible parts - and you'll achieve mastery over them all. You'll learn how to befriend, seduce, and resolve conflict with only the magic of communication. And by the end of your training, you'll know how to navigate nearly every situation known to man. From the difficult, strained scenarios to the intimate and deep connections.

Make no mistake, these skills will shake the foundation of your entire life. After all, the quality of our relationships is directly influenced by how well or how badly we communicate. It can mean the difference between constant fighting and empowering conversation. Or the difference between a dull interaction and smooth-talking your way into a life-changing opportunity. Our only warning? We hope you're ready for these newfound abilities.

## Conversation Skills

You see, communication is the closest thing to magic that exists. Once you master tone, language, timing, and a few other essential factors, you can produce any desired effect. The human mind is malleable, and except for the occasional idiosyncrasy, human needs are pretty easy to anticipate. Understanding them is the key to forming successful social strategies. You'll soon learn all about this.

I developed these advanced skills the hard way: through trial and error, through falling prey to the tactics of masters, and getting to know every personality type imaginable, no matter how aggravating. I studied the methods of a diverse range of people and learned from their mistakes as well as their successes. I said and did the wrong thing – but then I learned to say the right thing. And I perfected the right thing. I discovered when the right thing works best, when it doesn't work at all and when the right thing must give way to a better thing. I observed every move, every subtlety. And then I did extensive research to expand on what I already knew. I dissected the powerful areas of communication most people overlook; I will teach you to never overlook them again and how to use them to your fullest advantage.

I have watched fragile nobodies evolve into masters of persuasion with a presence that cannot be ignored. I am often thanked by people who have used my advice, with claims that it transformed their personal relationships, and helped them create new, more meaningful ones, as well. But it's no surprise that these benefits arise. Perfecting the art of conversation is synonymous with perfecting one's ability to live in tandem with other human beings. The people I've helped have become experts at both. I will be sharing these same secrets with you, very shortly.

With my help and expertise, you'll move past crippling shyness, dullness, and all breeds of social ineptitude. Instead, you'll spark fascinating interactions, deep connections and develop all the skills necessary to own every room you enter. You won't just open doors to new opportunities; you'll charm those doors right off their hinges. My guides will run the gamut, from seducing romantic interests to negotiating a better deal, children, difficult personalities, and more. You will need no other communication guide again. Consider this your conversation bible.

You've made that vital first step – now don't make the common mistake of ending the journey here. Remember this important fact: complacency is the silent killer of all potential. What doors are you allowing to shut while you sit idly?

As you reveal this book's next chapter, so shall you unveil *your* new chapter. Welcome to the only communication guide you'll ever need.

Conversation Skills

# Chapter 1 - Establishing Likability

Imagine this: a man saunters into the party you're attending. He's dressed exceptionally well in a crisp, button-down shirt, smart casual pants, and polished leather shoes. He makes eye contact with everyone in the room for a brief moment, smiling occasionally, and gesturing a friendly hello to someone he recognizes. His body is open towards the room, and he's even nodding his head slightly to the rhythm of the music playing in the background. The woman you're talking to - your new acquaintance, Claire - notices him. She waves and beams, and he does the same. He looks between you both, surveying the situation, and then he comes over slowly, ready to introduce himself with a warm smile.

Before he's even said a word, this man has established himself as a likable person. There's a high likelihood that you already feel comfortable letting him join your conversation. You may even feel the desire to get to know him and consider him as a potential friend. It's true that you don't really know who he is, and it's possible he could be the opposite of what you expect – but the point is, you want to find out. And because he's displayed likable behavior, he's already at an advantage.

## The Confirmation Bias

When we have a preexisting idea or belief, we tend to only notice factors that can confirm our assumptions. This idea forms the crux of the confirmation bias. In other words, you see what you want to see to confirm your initial judgment was correct. Humans enjoy being right. And so we absorb information selectively to prove our point, not disprove it.

## Conversation Skills

How does this play into our scenario with the likable man? Let's say you finally speak to him, and he mistakenly assumes he's met you before and calls you by the wrong name. This would be a social flub on his part, but if you'd already established that you think he's likable, you'd probably let it slide easily. In fact, you'd probably think, "Oh, it's a simple mistake. It happens sometimes and you can't help it. I'm sure he meets a lot of people." You'd then forget it and instead choose to remember how kind he was when he apologized.

But consider this other scenario: let's say, it was a different man, and he walked into the room with a scowl and a tight jaw. When he looked around the room, his eyes lingered a bit too long and inappropriately on a good-looking woman, and when he noticed your friend, he raised his eyebrows and didn't smile. If the same occurrence happened where he called you by the wrong name, you probably wouldn't be so forgiving. You'd maybe think, "Clearly he doesn't really respect people." You would choose to remember the mistake he made, and even if he apologized, chances are you'd be harder to win over.

In both scenarios, you're only looking to confirm what you already believe – but you could be completely wrong about both assumptions. The first man could turn out to be an arrogant narcissist and the second man could turn out to be intelligent and kind, just very socially awkward. The problem is, we'd only know for sure if we sat down and got to know these men on a deeper level. But most social interactions don't grant us that much time and chances are, you've already decided you don't want to get to know the unlikable man.

This is why we must emphasize likable behavior. People are assessing whether they like or don't like you, and whether they want to get to know you or not, as soon as you walk in the room. And this will greatly influence all proceeding interactions. You may have a great personality, but no one will ever know about it if your behavior comes across as cold, awkward, or uninviting. Start off on the right foot and send positive signals.

## The Qualities & Behaviors that Make You Instantly Likable

### 1. An Impressive Appearance

Contrary to popular belief, an impressive appearance doesn't just consist of good looks or expensive clothing. It encompasses everything about the way we carry and present ourselves to the world. It includes:

- The way you dress

Dressing well does not always mean formal. In fact, a necessary part of dressing well is making sure you've dressed appropriately for the occasion. If someone arrives at a low-key social gathering in a sharp suit for no reason, they may be perceived as pretentious. Conversely, if it's a formal event and you attend wearing sneakers, you'll be seen as sloppy and not taking it seriously.

People who dress sharply for every occasion (this means fitted, neat, and appropriate clothing) will always command more respect than someone who doesn't care at all about what they're wearing. Why? Not only does it send the message that you're intelligent and competent, it also tells people, "I am extremely socially aware and I have the means to take care of myself."

- The way you speak

Do you mumble or slur your words? Do you laugh nervously between sentences? Or do you enunciate and speak at just the right pace? The way you speak is a reflection of many important attributes. It will determine greatly how people perceive you and better yet, the

## Conversation Skills

way others will choose to interact with you. If your voice is too soft and slow, you will get overpowered. Studies have shown that those who display quiet voices give off the impression of being weak and inexperienced. At the opposite end, however, a voice that is high-pitched and loud is perceived to be unreliable, arrogant, and impatient. The ideal voice is firm, well-defined, and at a medium pace and volume. Even if you're saying a simple greeting, project the voice that suits the message you want to send.

### 2. Open and Interested Body Language

Your gestures and stances are sending messages as well. You may not be aware of it, but every person who encounters you will respond to the positioning of your body. To enhance your likability, it's imperative that you display a sense of openness.

- <u>Turn towards the person you're speaking to</u>

Your face may be angled towards your conversation partner, but what about the rest of your body? When you're turned away, your body language could be interpreted as uninterested or nervous. Facing them squarely, however, will make you appear invested and interested in the conversation. This, in turn, will make people more inclined to engage with you.

- <u>Gesture with your hands or let your arms hang loose</u>

People tend to overlook what their arms are doing when they're conversing, but this is another tell-tale sign of how a person feels. Arms that are tight and locked give the impression of someone insecure or rigid. To appear more likable, let them hang loose and if you can, gesture as you speak. People tend to respond well to someone who is expressive with their hands. This will demonstrate that you're comfortable, confident and enthusiastic about the situation at hand.

## Conversation Skills

- Mirror your conversation partner's behavior

Humans have a deep need to make connection with someone else. An effective way to ignite feelings of connection is to mimic someone's behavior in conversation. When they say something and smile, try smiling too. If they take a sip of their drink, you should as well. This will make the other party feel that you're in alignment with them, like you're on the same page. However, for mirroring to work successfully, it's important that you don't do it for the entire length of the conversation as this will seem unnatural and the other person will likely notice. Psychologists also advise not mirroring right away. If a conversation has not had time to find its rhythm, any conscious mimicry will be seen as such.

- Loose and upright posture

We all know that standing straighter conveys a more appealing impression, but that's not all there is to it. Our posture must also be fairly loose, as this tells people we're welcoming and comfortable. People who stand straight and rigidly tend to seem unapproachable and sometimes even severe.

### 3. Looking Happy to Be There

When a person looks happy to be where they are, they look comfortable and safe to be around. When we encounter someone who appears this way, we instinctively feel comfortable too, and we sense that their company must be pleasant. This is similar to displaying open body language, but not entirely the same. Open body language will say we're available, but a happy and pleasant aura will actually send the invitation.

- Smiling just the right amount

The most recognizable signal for happiness is the smile, and it's an easy way to convey your pleasure. Keep a relaxed smile on your face and you'll find that more people start interacting with you. Smile at the appropriate intervals when someone is telling a story and smile when you see someone that you know. Just be careful to not grin too much or too widely if it's not entirely genuine. A fake smile can be alarming and creepy, and may produce an adverse effect.

- <u>Make sure your neutral expression is relaxed and pleasant</u>

Many of us lose control of our neutral expressions. We think we look perfectly normal, but other people might still think we're unapproachable. Have you ever seen someone with Resting Bitch Face (RBF)? Exactly. Stay aware of what your neutral expression is. Even if you're just wandering over to the snack table to grab more finger food, keep your expression relaxed, with the corners of your mouth upturned ever so slightly. This is not a full on smile, but it conveys the message that you're happy to be there.

## What Determines Likable Behavior?

Likable behavior is not made up of a random set of traits and actions, they can all be drawn down to the same basic needs. We search for basic assurances in every single person we encounter and this will determine how positively we respond to them as well as how likely we are to seek their company again. If you keep your conversation partners' three basic needs in mind, you may find yourself displaying likable behavior naturally.

- Safety

You may not realize this, but a number of qualities we search for, such as approachability and trustworthiness, can all be attributed to our desire for safety. The basic animal nature in us all wants to ensure that we'll receive no threats to our well-being. It's not just about our physical safety, but our sense of self as we know it. We want to avoid emotional and mental threats, just as we want to avoid a physical threat. When a person displays approachability or trustworthiness, they are essentially saying 'You're safe around me.' Once our brains pick up this signal, we relax and open ourselves to the possibility of connection.

- Significance

Once we establish we're safe, we soften to the idea of connecting, but we're not there immediately. We also want to feel significant and important on some level. It's not enough that a person is approachable. If they aren't really listening to what we're saying, or they're always looking over our shoulder cause they are waiting for an opportunity to talk to someone else, chances are we won't be entirely impressed. Even if someone is smiling and acting very kind, we can always sense when our presence is truly valued and desired. Naturally, we want to be where we are appreciated.

- Expansion

A new acquaintance has successfully made us feel comfortable and significant in their presence – but there's still something missing. The cherry on top of the cake is expansion and an opportunity for growth. The desire to evolve and become better than we are is a natural human need. The solution to this need can take many forms, but it all comes down to a feeling of excitement and positive challenge.

When we meet someone that entertains us and stimulates us intellectually, our need for mental and emotional expansion is fulfilled. This need also encompasses humor since what we find truly funny, subconsciously tickles our intellect. We've all encountered jokes that we consider "too dumb" or jokes we just "don't get."

This is the hardest need to take care of since personal taste can play a large role here. It is also important to note that people who can take care of each other's needs for expansion are usually from roughly the same IQ level. What one person finds interesting can be extremely boring or confusing to another person.

## The Seven Bad Habits that are Making You Unlikable

Remember the unlikable guy from earlier? He's displaying a myriad of social turn-offs that are sending the wrong messages.

But do you want to know a terrifying thought? You, too, have definitely made some of those mistakes before. In fact, you might even make them to this day. Let's examine some classic and lesser known social mistakes, so you can start becoming more likable right now.

1. **Constantly on the Phone**

No one should feel bad for glancing at their phone or typing a quick text message, but in this modern day and age, such restraint is rare. If you have your phone out constantly, and are seen scrolling through social media while in the company of other people, you're going to leave a bad impression. Being absorbed by your device when other people expect you to stay present is seen as extremely rude. Would you start reading a book in the middle of a social gathering? Any decent person wouldn't, and this is not much different to frequent phone distractions. Save this behavior for when you're by yourself or at a very casual hang-out.

If you're expecting a call or trying to resolve something important via text, do so in another room. Or alternatively, apologize to the people you're with and explain how you're dealing with an important matter. This advice also applies to loud phone conversations in public. Find another room or lower your voice.

2. **Slouching or Slumping in Your Seat**

Unless you're at your best friend's house for a casual hang-out, slouching or slumping in your seat sends the signal that you're either lazy or submissive. To people you don't know, it can even convey a complete lack of interest in what they're saying. By slouching or slumping, you make your body appear smaller, and instinctively we interpret this as a lack of confidence and power.

### 3. Inappropriate or Lack of Eye Contact

Watching what someone does with their eyes is a great way to get a good read on them. Are they displaying judgment by looking everyone up and down? Are they being misogynistic by staring at women inappropriately? Or are they awkward and standoffish, making no eye contact at all? All of the above are examples of what can turn us off a new acquaintance. Avoid making those mistakes.

### 4. Bad Hygiene

When someone smells bad or looks like they haven't washed themselves in days, they're saying, "I can't take care of myself." As intelligent animals who are interested in self-preservation, we are wired to be repelled by something that we think is dirty. Subconsciously we associate it with breeding grounds for organisms and diseases that could threaten our well-being. Even if we know a person isn't diseased, the self-preserving animal in us has learned to have this reaction to potentially unsanitary situations, objects, or people.

Of course, no one stops caring for a friend or loved one because they have bad hygiene, but it is the reason we have the urge to hold our nose and sit further away from them. These reactions are not conducive to positive social interactions.

This reflex is hardwired into us in the same way we can't help but blink and produce tears when a foreign particle gets into our eyes.

## Conversation Skills

These are ways the living body has learned to cope with potential threats.

For this reason, most people (except for those who already live in unsanitary conditions) are repelled by bad hygiene. While it's perfectly normal to have a sweaty day now and then, where you may not smell as fresh as you usually do, consistent grime will make it difficult for you to charm anyone.

### 5. Not Participating in Conversations

Being mysterious is one thing, but if you are always seen staying completely silent in social settings, this can make you seem unfriendly or even dim-witted. When reserved people are in the presence of their outgoing friends, it comes naturally to let the talkers do the talking, but they should resist this urge. Even if it's just a one-liner or a question here and there, make sure you are contributing something to every conversation you're involved in. It's really quite simple: if you don't offer anything, you look like you have nothing to offer.

### 6. Not Dressing Appropriately

Remember what we said about dressing well for every occasion? Not everyone has a great sense of style, and that's okay, but at the very least, you must make sure you dress appropriately. This applies to men and women. Save your skimpy skirts and surfer tank tops for parties with your good friends, but never wear them to formal events or first-time meetings with your significant other's parents. Keep this in mind: always dress in alignment with the message you want to send to the room.

### 7. Not Respecting Personal Space

Personal space is more than just getting in someone's way or touching someone you don't know well. It encompasses behavior like cutting in front of a stranger in line, going through someone's belongings without permission, or entering someone's bedroom, office, or house without knocking first. Even actions that are intended to be friendly, like forcibly hugging someone you don't know, can be experienced as a violation of personal space. It depends on whether you were given verbal or nonverbal consent to enter someone's space or touch their property (and this includes their body).

Always respect the privacy of others, and their right to refuse physical contact. Anyone who witnesses such an invasion will see you as disrespectful and socially inept.

Never lose track of the way you present yourself to the world, whether physically or behaviorally. A conversation is far more than our verbal communications; it's also about what we say with our actions and responses. To truly master conversation skills, you must conquer the art of likable behavior.

# Chapter 2 - The Basics of Good Conversation

You've learned how to behave in public, but the journey is far from over. As soon as you open your mouth to enter a conversation, you're in a different arena and a new set of skills comes into play. Our image is one thing, but as soon as this phase of communication begins, people finally get to see how that image stacks up against what we say and how we say it. Are we all that we portray ourselves to be? Are we as impressive as the words on our resume? Are we as classy as the way we dress?

## How to Make Great First Impressions

You may think that short interactions are easier to pull off, but that could not be less true. Unlike sit-down chats or long conversations, you have a shorter amount of time to win the other party over. If you behave awkwardly or say something you shouldn't have, before you know it time's up, and that's how they'll remember you from now onwards. You have one try and then it's over until the next meeting, if it even exists.

Learning to master first impressions and small talk are crucial for many life-shaping events. A potential new employer doesn't have time or the interest to get to know you in depth, you need to charm him in a short amount of time. And the same rule applies to that cute boy or girl you run into sometimes. You need to make a good impression before you get that date.

To turn that one-time encounter into something more, here are some essential tips:

- **Butter up your introduction**

Don't just say 'My name is Peter,' say 'My name is Peter, it's really nice to meet you.' You'd be surprised by how simple a sentence can take your first impression up a few notches. This will immediately warm any new person to you, as you've successfully made them feel important, interesting, and like you want to continue being around them. We've established that humans enjoy feeling safe and significant; this is an easy, simple way to tick both those boxes immediately.

- **Learn how to give a good handshake**

Many potential employers and professional connections pay attention to the way you shake their hand. Keep in mind these three major factors: the strength of your grip, the duration, and the positioning of your hand.

The perfect handshake is not too soft, not too tight, but perfectly firm. You should shake their hand for two to three pumps, for no more than three seconds, but ideally two seconds. During the handshake, your arm should also be perfectly vertical. Never show the underside of your wrist or the top of your forearm, as this shows submission or dominance respectively.

Please note that if you shake hands with an individual who puts your hand on the bottom, with your wrist exposed, this means they are making a power play. If they pull you towards them as they shake your hand, they are also performing a power move. These are classic signs of exerting dominance. We don't advise making these power plays on other people, unless you are prepared for some tension.

- **Be considerate**

There's a good reason this encounter is brief. Perhaps you're talking to someone while they're at work, between meetings, or at a crowded social event. Whatever the scenario, be considerate of other peoples' time and attention. Consider the circumstances and question at what point you might become an intrusion. Are you trying to talk to someone while they're working? Or perhaps they're on their short lunch break and you're holding them up in the office corridor? Don't insist on holding a person's attention for a long time, when you know you're not the only reason they're there.

- **Make eye contact**

During quick encounters, many people shy away from eye contact. Whether it's due to social awkwardness or because you've been caught by surprise, resist the urge to let this discomfort be seen. Make sufficient eye contact with the person you're speaking with, but also resist the urge to stare. Look directly at them as they speak.

## Conversation Skills

For one-on-one conversations, you should break eye contact every 7-10 seconds. For group settings, however, try and break eye contact between 4-6 seconds.

- **Ask a question to show you're interested**

It's a quick chat, sure, but it's fine to shoot off a question as long as it's easy to answer and they aren't in a rush to get anywhere. This shows that you're interested and curious about them, since you chose to ask a question when you didn't have to. This is even more important for job interviews since employers expect questions, and will even judge prospective employees based on the questions they ask. Whatever the situation, make sure the questions you ask during brief encounters are not too personal or time-consuming.

- **Don't be *too* honest when you answer the question "How are you?"**

There are some individuals with which we *can* be honest about how we're doing – but they're all people we already know well, in which case, we are long past the stage of worrying about first-impressions. With the rest, however, it's best to keep it light and positive. Even if you're going through a difficult period in your life, understate it in a way that the other person doesn't suddenly feel they have to ask what's wrong and console you. Say something like, "I've been better, but I'm sure things will look up soon." Often when people ask you how you are, they're doing so out of politeness and good social decorum. Save your long, honest answers for your good friends and family. And always remember to ask the other person the same question!

- **Use environmental triggers**

If you can't think of a single thing to say, look around you. There's material everywhere! If you're running into someone at a grocery store, you could ask if they shop there often. If the encounter takes place at the train station, you could share where you're going and ask where they're headed as well. If the person in question is wearing something particularly striking, compliment them! Look around you in the moment and you'll realize there's a lot to talk about.

- **Give an uplifting goodbye**

Sometimes you get lucky and the person you've run into is someone you want to see again soon. You may make plans and part with a happy, "See you on Tuesday!" Most of the time, however, you're probably running into someone you don't care to see again, or someone you're not sure you'll see again, such as a prospective employer. To make the best impression, send them off with some positive and uplifting parting words. Tell them "Have a great day!" or give them well wishes in regards to what they've shared with you. For example, "Good luck with your marathon!" or "Have a great time at dinner!"

Conversation Skills
# Win at Small Talk with the ARE Model

If you want a simple, easy formula for good small talk, this section is for you. Carol Fleming, a communications expert and coach, created a three-point method for helping individuals get better at small-talk. This plan works on shy and confident folks alike. ARE stands for:

- **Anchor** – To begin, find something that you are your conversation partner both have in common in the current moment. Fleming describes this as your "shared reality." Look around and see what you notice. It could be anything from the food being served or someone in an outrageous outfit that you can both see. Anchoring involves choosing a focus and stating the observation. For example, let's say you're making small talk at a fancy party. You tell a new acquaintance: "These appetizers are delicious."

- **Reveal** – Then comes something about you. Share a slightly personal tidbit that's relevant to the topic you've just brought up. It doesn't have to be complicated or mind-blowing. This is just to establish the dynamic of sharing with each other. You could say, "I wish I could make something like this, but I'm just not very skilled in the kitchen."

- **Encourage** – Finally, you give your acquaintance an opening to respond. Focus on being friendly and encouraging so that they share information about themselves with you. This should take the form of a question. An idea is: "Are you a good cook? You look like someone with a lot of hidden talents!"

Whenever you're feeling nervous or more unsteady than usual, remember this formula to get yourself back into the small-talk groove. Don't shy away from small talk. It's the precursor to a long, engaging conversation with a potential new friend or professional connection. It is the first step that leads to all other steps. Keep these tools in mind to start winning at small talk.

## Three Essential Ways to Get Along with Anyone You Meet

We all know someone with seemingly irresistible charm; someone who's liked by everyone they meet, no matter the personality type and no matter the circumstance. The trick to getting along with others is not rocket science, but it does require a big mental and behavioral shift. We might have already displayed likable behavior, earning the interest of a new conversation partner, but now we need to know how to sustain this interest. Now that someone has given us the chance to get to know them, we need a new set of skills to create conversational harmony.

### 1. Show Genuine Interest in Others

It seems simple, doesn't it? And yet you'd be surprised by how many fail this basic step. Showing genuine interest requires more than just

## Conversation Skills

nodding and smiling. Remember the basic social need for significance? The person you're conversing with must feel that you care about what they're saying and who they are. We all want to feel as though we are valued and appreciated. These behaviors can demonstrate genuine interest:

- Ask questions. Get to know the person you're conversing with better, but make sure to do so in a way that is not interrogative, and steer clear of questions that are too personal unless you know them well. If they are telling you about an activity they enjoy, ask them why they like it, or when they started.

- Pay attention. When someone is talking, stay present and listen to what they're saying. Most people can sense when the person they're talking to has zoned out of the conversation, and this is a major social turn off. Why would you want to talk to someone who isn't listening? You wouldn't. If someone is telling a story, try to paint a mental picture with the details they're giving you. A good trick is to imagine what they're saying as a movie.

- Show enthusiasm. When someone talks to you, don't just nod and blink like a fool. Smile, look receptive, and when they share new information with you, show enthusiasm. When necessary, respond with phrases like, "Wow, that's very interesting!" or "How wonderful. That's great to hear." People always respond well to enthusiastic positivity.

## 2. Be Kind

People who display kindness are pleasant to be around: that's a fact. We instinctively feel safe around them and develop trust for them. An act or word of kindness can easily brighten up a day, and it's an important step to getting along with someone. You'll be hard pressed to find someone who isn't won over by kindness. Here are some ideas for showing your nice side:

- Display good manners. That's right, everything your parents taught you about saying please and thank you, holding open the door, respecting personal space, and all the rest, are all valuable social skills. Manners display consideration for other people. The reason we are taught this when we are young is because this is the most basic form of human kindness. Display good manners and you'll start off on the right foot.

- Empathize. This doesn't mean you have to listen to someone's problems and hold their hand; we can always empathize, even over small matters. Perhaps, you're at a formal dinner and someone's food gets forgotten. Say something like, "I'm so sorry you have to wait. It's always annoying when food doesn't arrive on time." It's simple, but filled with empathy. The other person will immediately feel

## Conversation Skills

like you care about them, and will be highly receptive to anything else you might say.

### 3. Open Up

Remember our need for expansion? It's not enough to be kind and receptive, we should also show our conversation partners that we have something to offer them. We do this by opening up, talking about ourselves, and responding to what they say in a thoughtful, informative or entertaining manner.

- Share your experiences. The best part of this is it can be anything that delights you to share. The only requirements are that it is appropriate and doesn't dominate the entire conversation for an extended period of time. You can share anything, from a funny encounter you had that day to a fascinating experience you had abroad. Keep it interesting and leave out the unnecessary details. When we share stories with others, it allows them to get to know us and invites them to see what is interesting about us.

- Share an interesting thought, feeling, or observation. If you don't have any relevant experiences to share, or you simply can't think of anything, then try to respond to your current surroundings or the conversation at hand. Ideally, it would be something that reflects your personal taste or an opinion you hold. They want to get to know you, remember?

## Six Tips for Resisting Shyness and a Lack of Confidence

Some of you can't help it – you're shy, and that's just the way you are. You're more wary of people, and you've never understood how chatterboxes can so freely interact with others they don't know. Even if you have the desire to socialize, you end up not contributing very much to the conversation. Sometimes this is because you have social anxiety and a lack of confidence, and other times, it's just because you're more reserved than the average person.

There's nothing wrong with being shy or reserved, but you'll definitely encounter situations in your life where you'll need to talk more than you're comfortable with. Perhaps you're talking to a prospective employer, or maybe you're meeting a significant other's parents for the first time. To safeguard against awkward moments and silences, keep these tips in mind:

1. **Prepare beforehand**

If you're nervous about an upcoming social interaction, there's nothing wrong with preparing for it in advance. Think of interesting stories to tell, and perhaps even practice the way you want to tell them. If you're feeling confident, prepare some jokes. Make sure you know them well but try not to over-rehease, or they won't sound natural.

## Conversation Skills

If you already know about potential conversation topics that the other person will bring up, it's also a great idea to think of how you will respond. For example, if you're about to spend time with someone who recently did a lot of traveling, think of an interesting travel experience that you've had, and practice telling the story in an amusing way. Use what you know about the people you're spending time with to come up with great conversation topics and stories.

If you're about to meet your significant other's parents for the first time, and you know they'll ask you about your career or where you grew up, think of engaging and relevant stories that you can share with them. To be extra prepared, come up with a list of questions to ask whenever there is a lull in the conversation.

Planned interactions can turn out extremely well, and the best part is, you'll feel a lot more confident afterwards.

**2. Focus away from yourself**

If you dread being the center of attention, this is a tip for you. There are many ways to direct the spotlight onto someone else. One sure way is to ask lots of questions. Instead of staying silent, try to learn about someone else. This will reflect upon you positively as you'll also appear curious and interested, two qualities that people tend to be drawn to. You won't have to feel vulnerable, and yet you're still participating in the conversation.

To keep attention off yourself for as long as possible, make sure to ask open-ended questions, not just something that can be answered with a 'yes' or 'no.' If you meet someone from a foreign place, ask them what it's like where they are from, and if you're speaking with a work acquaintance, ask them what they like to do on the weekends. To successfully avoid the spotlight, think of more questions to keep the conversation evolving. Otherwise, the other person will likely ask "How about you?" if silence presents itself.

### 3. Focus on connecting, not impressing

During moments of anxiety, people tend to forget that it's more important to connect than it is to impress. If you focus on impressing, you'll most likely come across as trying too hard and making all the wrong moves. People can sense when someone is actively trying to impress, and this tends to produce a negative reaction. What you should focus on is genuine connection. Get to know the other person, empathize with them, and don't be afraid to give them a genuine compliment. Instead of thinking about all the ways you can show off, really listen to what they're saying and respond in a thoughtful manner. Try to also discover your common interests.

### 4. Don't be someone you're not

Shy people should never forget this fact. In the pursuit of better conversation skills, it can be easy to feel like you're trying to be someone else, but it's important to remember it's not like that at all. It's not about giving yourself qualities that you don't have, it's about developing enough confidence to share the qualities you possess with other people. Shy people should never feel the need to pretend they're extroverted or gregarious people. It's about getting used to including your great qualities and interesting experiences in the wider conversation.

There are many ways that people pretend to be someone they are not. Sometimes this manifests in false stories and lies, and sometimes even fake personas and forced behavior. If you find yourself doing this, your attempt at socializing will backfire. Fake people attract other fake people, and this will repel meaningful connections.

### 5. Recognize that you have something to contribute

We've all lived unique lives and we need to recognize there's something about all of us that makes us interesting. No one has lived exactly the same life as you. You may share the same hometown, the same parents, or even a similar trauma to someone else, but no one possesses the same combination of upbringing, experiences, and choices as you. This means you're unique and you have something to contribute that no one has ever heard before. You need to recognize that you have valuable insights. You may feel shy or reserved, but consider the fact that other people in the conversation might benefit from hearing your point of view.

### 6. Understand that not everyone is as confident as they seem

You're not alone. Chances are high that even the person you're talking to is fighting their shier urges. While there certainly are many extroverted and socially comfortable people out there, the majority of people identify as an introvert. Even wildly successful individuals

## Conversation Skills

like Mark Zuckerberg and Steven Spielberg are known to have shy and anxious tendencies. Yet you'd never guess it with the number of public appearances they've both made and, most importantly, with how confident they come across. Know that you, too, can seem this confident, even if you don't feel that way deep down inside.

# Chapter 3 - Igniting Exceptional Interactions

You've made it past first impressions and you've pulled them into a full on conversation. Now what? At this point, many people find themselves at a loss for words, unsure of what exactly to say next. You've already asked them how they've been, what they did over the summer, and told them how great their outfit is. Now, they're looking at you expectantly and you have no idea how to fill the silence.

We all crave engaging discussions and a genuine bond, but when you're standing in that silence, it can feel impossible. How can we make what we say mean something? What can we do to break away from hum-drum hellos and how-do-you-dos? How can we be interesting conversationalists?

## Conversation Topics & Tips for Every Possible Scenario

Depending on the exact circumstances, certain topics may be more or less appropriate for the occasion. Nevertheless, there are a great deal of topics that can ignite fascinating discussion, regardless of context.

For the most successful delivery, it's advised to work in new topics as naturally as possible instead of simply blurting out a question. For best results, try and include an interesting story or observation that is relevant to the topic.

**Friends**

We should feel comfortable around our friends, but there are many scenarios in which we might not. For example, with new friends. Or perhaps, if you're talking one-on-one with a friend that you normally see with a group. Dynamics also change depending on how many people are involved, and it's wise to adjust communication methods to the exact context.

With groups, it's a good idea to ask questions that give everyone the opportunity to contribute and share. Asking overly personal questions in a group setting may make someone feel put on the spot, and it's likely the whole group doesn't want to slow down to listen to one person's story for a long time. Keep questions, in these scenarios, open to everyone.

When you're in a one-on-one talk, on the other hand, conversation can be highly engaging if you ask them questions you wouldn't normally ask. Take a look at these examples for some ideas:

<u>New Friends</u>

- How long have you known each other and how did you meet?
- What does everyone think about that latest episode in [insert TV show here]?
- What did everyone do last weekend?

## Conversation Skills

- Does anyone have any funny bad date stories?
- What is everyone binging on Netflix right now?
- What's the craziest thing you've seen on the news recently?
- Has anyone here ever met a celebrity? If so, what happened?
- What's the most trouble you've ever gotten into?
- If your life story was turned into a movie and this moment made it into a scene, who would play you and who would you choose to play everyone else?
- How would you say you've changed since High School?

<u>One-on-One Conversations</u>

- How is work going?
- Are you seeing anyone these days?
- What do you think of [random mutual friend]'s new girlfriend/boyfriend?
- How often do you see your family?
- What's the most embarrassing thing that's ever happened to you?
- Do you consider yourself an introvert or an extrovert?
- How many relationships have you had and which one shaped you the most?
- What's the worst sexual experience you've ever had?
- What are some goals you're currently trying to achieve?
- Have you ever gotten into a physical fight?
- Which world cultures are you most fascinated by?

**Work Acquaintances**

There will be a range of intimacy levels with work acquaintances. Some you may be very comfortable with while others feel distant. Regardless of how well you get along, it's always best to keep conversations with colleagues somewhat professional. This doesn't mean that all talks need to be stiff and formal, it simply means they should remain within a narrow realm of topics. With the exception of rare circumstances, questions that are personal will not be seen as appropriate.

- If you didn't have this job, what would you be doing instead?
- What do you like to do on the weekends?
- How do you recharge after a long workday?
- Do you have any tricks for making it through a stressful workday?
- What's the weirdest job you've ever had?
- Have you ever had a crush on a coworker?
- If you could have lunch with anyone in the world, who would it be?

**Family**

Unlike our friends and romantic partners, we don't choose our family. And shared DNA doesn't always mean shared interests. It's not uncommon for family time to be awkward. Whether it's your family or someone else's family you're spending time with, one thing is for sure: family topics are always welcome. A great conversation starter is to ask about a specific family story, or question them about their earlier family life. This can spark a fascinating story and the chosen family member will feel touched by your curiosity.

<u>Your Family</u>

- Do we have any precious family heirlooms?
- What's our ancestry?
- What was your favorite pastime when you were a child?
- Do we have any interesting family secrets that I don't know about?
- Are we related to anyone famous?
- Who do you think I'm the most similar to in our family?
- What are some dominant familial traits?
- What's the most awkward moment you've ever seen at a family gathering?
- What was the first job you ever had?
- What are some of the biggest ways the world has changed since you were younger?
- What was [random family member] like when he/she was younger?
- How did [married family members] meet? (also feel free to ask this question directly to the subjects)

**Romantic**

There is a little more wiggle room when it comes to conversations with a romantic interest. This is because both parties are often

## Conversation Skills

actively trying to get to know each other, so questions that would normally seem out-of-the-blue are not that unusual. For example, if you're talking to a regular acquaintance and ask them, "How long was your longest relationship?" they may consider this question very personal and nosey. But on a date with a romantic interest, getting to know each other is expected. After all, you are trying to test how compatible you are.

- What are your guilty pleasures?
- Are you close with your family?
- Are you more like your mother or your father?
- What were you like as a teenager?
- How long was your longest relationship?
- How do you think you've changed in the last 10 years?
- What's your love language?
- Do you prefer fun nights out or cozy nights in?
- If you could settle down in any country in the world, which one would you choose?
- What's a movie, song, or book that has really shaped the way you see the world?
- What's your weirdest or most interesting habit?
- What's your favorite way to experience nature?
- What's your dream job?
- Who are your best friends and why?
- Do you consider yourself an introvert or an extrovert?
- What was the most challenging aspect of your childhood?

- How comfortable are you with public displays of affection?
- What would you consider a deal-breaker in a relationship or potential partner?

## The Worst Mistakes You Can Make in a Conversation

Once we begin actively talking to someone, there are many reasons the interaction could fall flat. It's not always for the reason you think and chances are, even though you think you're socially adept, you're making at least one of these mistakes.

### 1. Talking about yourself too much

If you come across as a narcissist, you can say goodbye to a genuine human connection. While people may enjoy learning about you, you shouldn't expect them to listen to long stories about your life without asking for theirs in return. It takes two to form a connection, and if there's no space for another person in the conversation, what's the point? If you notice yourself continuously changing the subject to you and your life, stop and ask your conversation partner something about their life. Listen carefully while they tell their story, and do not respond with something about yourself each time. Instead, try to acknowledge what they've said and extend understanding or an observation.

### 2. Acting like a know-it-all

Due to our need for expansion, we enjoy being around smart people. We don't, however, enjoy being around know-it-alls. You may be wondering what the difference is, and the answer is simple: know-it-alls are smart people who constantly feel the need to prove they're smart. Do you go on long tangents, explaining complex or obscure ideas to people who don't care and didn't ask for an explanation? Do you go out of your way to demonstrate your breadth of knowledge because you want recognition? You might be a know-it-all. This can be another form of narcissism but occasionally, it can signify a lack of-self esteem. Know-it-alls are sometimes so insecure that they latch onto the one trait they feel confident about, their intelligence. If this sounds like you, resist the urge to prove how smart you are all the time. This will only push people away. After all, if you're acting above them, how can they form a connection with you?

### 3. Being pedantic

Pedantry can sometimes signify a know-it-all, but not all the time. Even unintelligent people can be pedantic. What makes a pedant? Someone who is overly concerned with unimportant details and rules. They will go out of their way to correct people about trivial facts, even if it has no bearing on the conversation.

Let's say you're telling a new acquaintance about something amusing that happened to you and your friend, Rhonda, who is also present.

"We were just at a restaurant on 3rd and Geary Street," you begin to say, "And a woman asked for my autograph. Turns out she mistook me for a celebrity!"

You and your new acquaintance laugh, but Rhonda says, "Actually, the restaurant was on 3rd and Brady, not Geary." In this scenario, Rhonda is being pedantic. This detail is not important to the story, but she had to chime in anyway. After this comment, there is likely to be an awkward pause in the conversation. Don't interrupt the good mood for an insignificant detail. Avoid the urge to correct people if it makes no difference to the conversation. Let it go!

### 4. Oversharing

We all want to form an emotional connection. Intimate friendships or relationships can be great catalysts for this. When you share information that is too personal with someone you are not close to, however, this is called oversharing. Let's turn to socially awkward Rhonda again. She's meeting up with a new friend for the first time and they're having a casual lunch in town. She realizes that it's Monday the 3rd, and she suddenly remembers that her parents got divorced on Monday the 3rd many years ago. She begins telling her new friend all about the trauma she endured when her parents became divorced.

The new friend has just been on the receiving end of oversharing. Rhonda doesn't know her new friend that well yet, and she has already started sharing something extremely personal. This puts the other party in an uncomfortable place because they are still casually getting to know you, but now they feel they need to console you.

Save your personal stories for after you know a person reasonably well.

### 5. Being pretentious

Pretentiousness is very common, and we're all guilty of it sometimes. We can be pretentious for many reasons. Perhaps, we want to look more cultured, more popular, or just generally more interesting. A know-it-all can also be classified as being pretentious if their intention is to impress someone. A pretentious person tends to enjoy showing off and exaggerating some aspect of themselves. They may want to impress people by demonstrating they've read obscure books that most people don't understand, or perhaps they are constantly name-dropping famous people they've met to seem more influential. Whatever it is they're trying to demonstrate, no one likes a pretentious person. This is because pretentious people are playing a game, and others can sense it. Since people respond more positively to honesty and sincerity, pretentiousness can ruin your chances at getting someone to like you.

### 6. Not paying attention

We've all met someone like this. Sometimes they are narcissists who can't stop talking about themselves, but other times they may just appear disinterested and distracted. However it manifests, we've all had a conversation with someone who doesn't seem to be listening to what we're saying. It seems as if they're only waiting for their chance to respond. Not listening to our conversation partner is a major social faux pas. The other person can always tell and even if they don't show it, it's probably annoying them.

## 7. Preaching and lecturing

We tend to associate this kind of behavior with our parents or teachers – if you don't want your new friends to think of you as a nagging and annoying presence, then stay away from all forms of preaching and lecturing. Judgmental people can be prone to this kind of behavior, but other times it can be the result of attempted helpfulness gone wrong. It occurs when one party feels they know the best course of action on a particular subject, and instead of talking to their peers about it as an equal, they end up talking *at* them. Someone who engages in this behavior will constantly try to tell people what they 'should' do, and ramble on in the same way a parent does.

If you disagree with something an acquaintance or friend did, try asking questions to incite reflection. Or perhaps share a similar experience that you've had or heard of, and explain what the consequences were. Do this in a gentle and compassionate manner. There are many ways to make a suggestion without preaching.

## 8. Being easy to offend

The modern day has opened up many important conversations about the way we treat each other. Some people, however, have taken this a little too far. They insist on being offended even by minor things and will go out of their way to shove blame on anyone. If it's clear that no harm was intended, chill out and let it go. If someone says something ignorant out of a lack of knowledge instead of nastiness, gently enlighten them and then move on. People who are easily offended or upset cause others to feel as though they are walking on eggshells. And guess what? No one wants to talk to a person that makes them feel this way.

### 9. Talking badly about other people

It's a cheap trick to try and bond with someone. You don't know what else to talk about, so you try to connect with someone over mutual dislike for others. Sometimes it can even be a backwards way of complimenting the person you're talking to. For example, "You have such a beautiful home! Have you been to Jessica's house? Her decor is *so* tacky. And Kate's house is a total mess. You definitely have the nicest home of all." Unfortunately, this does work on some people, but this behavior is commonly associated with teenagers and high school politics. Friends who take on this dynamic encourage the worst parts of each others' personalities.

If you're looking to create a healthy connection that truly enriches your life, we don't advise talking badly about other people. Mature, secure, and emotionally stable individuals will immediately be repulsed by such behavior. If you are willing to talk this way about other people you know, there's little stopping you from talking this way about them.

## Conversation Skills
# Ideas to Steer Clear of Boring Conversations

Let's start off with a hard truth: some boring conversations cannot be prevented. Why? Because it takes more than one person to make it interesting. You can say all the right things and pull out the most effective techniques, but if the other person is obstinate and closed-off, then you can't control their behavior.

The good news is these instances are a rarity. Most shy and serious people can be pulled out of their shell with the right coaxing. Truth is, everyone has a humorous, interesting, or unusual side to them – you just have to find out how to access it.

1. **Share an embarrassing or unusual story**

Conversations become boring when no one is taking any risks. No one is sharing anything new, they're just saying what they feel they are supposed to say. When someone shares a genuine thought, feeling or observation, however, you'll notice your mind waking up. We are wired to find truth and honesty interesting, because it's something we can all connect with. It sends a signal that we can be ourselves. If you want to open up a new acquaintance and get them to expose a side of their personality they don't show anyone, you must create a safe environment for them. A great way to get the ball rolling is to share a story of your own. If it makes you seem a little vulnerable, they'll be far more engaged and likely to share something similar with you.

2. **Identify passions and ask about them**

## Conversation Skills

It's a no-brainer: everyone loves to talk about what they're passionate about. Listen out for what people say they enjoy and ask them for more details once you learn what it is. This might be someone's job, but not always since a lot of people don't really enjoy their jobs. To find out what these passions could be, pay attention to what people said they did on the weekends or don't be shy, just ask them what their favorite hobbies are!

### 3. Ask an open-ended question

You are completely within power to redirect the course of a conversation if you so desire. A great way to do this is by asking questions. Stay away from 'yes' or 'no' questions, however, since this will give people the opportunity to give a short answer. An open-ended question will force them to elaborate and take their answer to a more interesting place. Since they'll have to think more about their answer, they'll be more engaged in the conversation. Instead of the question "Do you enjoy your new job?" try asking "What is it like at your new job and what do you enjoy about it?" If all else fails, ask for their honest opinion on something.

### 4. Respond genuinely and elaborately

We've already established that people respond to honesty. That's why you should always respond to people genuinely, and without any pretenses. Please note that this is different from being brutally honest, where we may share an inappropriate or hurtful truth. Being genuine simply means we are not trying to be someone we are not. When we speak elaborately, we give the other person more to respond to.

### 5. Embrace your silly side

In other words, tell a joke every now and then. Bring some humor into the way you speak. Just keep it appropriate and mature, avoiding all humor that degrades another person. Silliness does not just mean silly faces or pranks (avoid this unless you're with good friends!) it means infusing a sense of the ridiculous into your conversation.

### 6. Lighten up

We all want to avoid boring conversations, but listen, don't stress yourself out. Chances are your conversation partners can tell when you're trying extremely hard. It may even manifest in over-seriousness or too much intensity which can put people off. Part of the trick is to just take it easy and enjoy yourself. Lighten up. Keep all these tips in mind but be natural and exude positivity, no matter how the conversation is going.

## Three General Rules for Sparking an Interesting Conversation

### 1. Bring up something *you* find interesting

One way we tend to sabotage a conversation is by only bringing up the topics we feel we're supposed to bring up. We stick to safe topics because we think that's what's expected of us. Unfortunately, this is a pretty common formula for a boring conversation – and why would you expect anything more than that? After all, even you don't really care about these topics, do you? To truly make a conversation interesting, bring up a topic you're actually fascinated by. There's a good chance that if you find it engaging, the other person will too.

## 2. Deepen conversation topics over time

It's completely normal to start off with a lighthearted topic. We all need to ease in. However, we can always make our conversations more interesting by taking them to a deeper level. And don't be scared of the word 'deep.' It doesn't mean you need to talk about existentialism or traumatic heartbreak. It just means that you need to get to the core of the subject and make it completely relatable.

For example, let's say two people start off talking about their cats and all the funny, adorable habits their little feline friends have. If they just stick to this aspect of their cats, they'll eventually run out of things to say. To keep things interesting, they need to take the topic to new depths. They should tell the stories of how they found their cats, complete with the emotions of it all, and they should discuss how it is that their cats bring so much to their lives. They could ponder interesting questions about pet-owner relationships, or what unique benefits a cat brings and a dog doesn't. Deepening a topic creates a bond. Try it in your next conversation.

## 3. Be as specific as possible

## Conversation Skills

Speaking in vague and general terms is a sure way to bore and frustrate your conversation partner. If someone asks you what you like to do on the weekends, don't just say, "I like to go out with friends." Give a more complete answer. When we offer up generalities, it doesn't give our conversation partners any material to respond to. This can result in awkwardness or strained conversation. It also sends the message that you're not very enthusiastic about the conversation at hand.

Instead of the above statement, say something more detailed like, "I like to go out with friends. We enjoy nightclub-hopping on the weekends and when that gets too much, we like to take road trips out into nature." The amended statement opens up two new doors: nightclubs and nature. Always aim to open new doors with your responses. Make it easy on your new acquaintances!

# Chapter 4 - Cultivating Charisma and Magnetism

It's one thing to have pleasurable conversations every now and then, but what if you want more than that? Some of us are blessed with charisma and magnetism. This means you don't have to pursue interesting interactions and people, instead they seem to find you. A small portion of people are gifted and naturally magnetic, but the rest of us shouldn't give up hope. Like most things in life, you don't have to be gifted to be good at something. You just need the self-awareness, knowledge, and the practice.

We've all met someone with charisma and magnetism. People are drawn to them like moths to light, purely because their presence is energizing and enjoyable. Magnetic individuals take communication skills to a new level entirely. They know which rules should be followed strictly, which ones should be broken, and which ones are exceptions in certain circumstances.

Magnetic individuals find it easier than most to achieve career success, large friend groups, and a wide variety of romantic options. The development of these qualities is no easy feat, but it can be done. First, however, you need to know the secrets.

Conversation Skills

# The Thirteen Secrets to Developing a Magnetic Personality

### 1. Cultivate emotional self-sufficiency

Arguably one of the most powerful qualities to develop, emotional self-sufficiency is a major driving force behind magnetic individuals. Quite simply, it signifies an ability to monitor your own emotions and needs, and understand exactly how to satisfy them without outside help. There is no dependence on other people to take care of their needs because they know how to do it themselves. They have mastered the teaching of 'You cannot control other people's actions, only your reactions' and they live closely by it. They focus on what they can control and nothing more. Other people are drawn to this quality because it makes a person seem stable, secure, and smart. We tend to trust someone who has control over their emotions as it gives the impression of maturity.

### 2. Your presence must give just as much as it takes

A truly magnetic personality does not operate from a 'me, me, me' philosophy. In fact, they make sure that other people in the conversation get something they need as well. Sometimes it's empathy, encouragement, gentle honesty, or even recognition. They are not afraid to compliment others, and when they do, it comes from a genuine place, instead of just wanting to score points. They might share interesting stories about themselves, but more than this, they are curious about other people, they ask questions, and they share

## Conversation Skills

comments that are both helpful and authentic. When people benefit from an interaction with you, whether it's mentally or emotionally, they are far more likely to seek your company again.

### 3. Learn to balance intelligence, humor and kindness

These three qualities are some of the most difficult to learn but when used in tandem, they can be irresistible. Intelligence allows us access to a large pool of data, humor makes it fun, and kindness creates the bond. People with strong magnetism utilize this trifecta to their advantage and with it, they charm people instantly.

### 4. Don't be afraid of vulnerability

Many people make the mistake of coming across too tough and impervious. Contrary to popular belief, this is not a good way to attract interesting connections. While it may temporarily impress or even intimidate people, it won't make anyone crave your company. This is because machismo or toughness is a pretense, and it will only attract people putting on the same pretense. Magnetic people are not afraid of being vulnerable. If it's relevant and appropriate, they have no issue sharing a heartfelt comment or allowing someone a glimpse into their true feelings. They do so in a manner that does not seek attention or overshare. People are drawn to this because we are engaged by sincerity.

### 5. Learn how to read people like a book

## Conversation Skills

It takes more than one person to create a successful social interaction. This is why a great communicator doesn't just focus on their own behavior, they also notice how others behave. They are masters at reading and interpreting signals to determine the mood of anyone around them. This skill is important because a person's mood can change constantly, and it will shape the way they perceive the world. This means that a persuasion tactic that works on happy Person A might not work on anxious Person B. Using what they gather from observation, magnetic people are able to adjust their tactics and behavior so as to elicit any desired response from anyone.

### 6. Stop publicizing everything

Magnetic people value privacy greatly, and you may even find that some of them carry an air of mystery. Do not try to become intentionally mysterious, as this is likely to backfire. Instead, learn to hold certain memories and experiences as sacred. Learn to see the value in privacy and stop publicizing everything about your life. Share deeply personal matters with a select few and resist blabbermouth tendencies. Someone who shares personal details incessantly comes across as overly-emotional and as having no control. These are qualities that tend to repel people instead of attracting them.

### 7. **Learn to adapt**

This valuable skill can only be learned through experience and trial-and-error. Once gained however, it will get you far. Magnetic individuals can adapt to a range of different scenarios and can get along with many kinds of people. Men, women, young, old, and even people from other cultures. They can pick up on the rhythm and communication style of their conversation partner, the type of stories they value, and they can adjust their behavior accordingly. At the end of the day, they know that whoever it is, you can always connect to the aspects of humanity that we all have in common.

### 8. Make the best of what makes you different

While there are certain social codes that are absolutely necessary, magnetic individuals are not fussed about total conformity. As long as they're dressed well and appropriately, they see no reason why they should wear the exact same style as everyone else. As long as they're being polite and considerate, why should they stick to the same hum-drum conversation topics that everyone else is discussing? Magnetic people won't go out of their way to stand out from a crowd, but they will embrace their natural eccentricities and proclivities.

### 9. Stop feeling embarrassed about every misstep

There are certain situations in which shame and embarrassment are deserved. For instance, if something mean we've said or something unethical we have done is exposed, then we should feel shame for those actions. But if no harm has been done or intended, a magnetic person rejects feelings of embarrassment. Why? Because, at the end of the day, only we can embarrass ourselves.

## Conversation Skills

Perhaps, you showed up to a party and are wearing the exact same outfit as another person. Consider these two opposite ways of reacting to this scenario:

- You sink into the nearest armchair and hope no one notices you. You immediately start telling your friend, "I can't believe it! I need to leave or find a new outfit." As you talk, you and your friend continue to look at this person, and they notice. Your face turns red, and everything about your body language says you don't want to be seen. The other party attendees notice the similar clothes, and since you are noticeably embarrassed, they are embarrassed for you. It affects your interactions for the rest of the night, as people are turned off by your awkward behavior.

- You notice the person in the same clothes and can't help but see the amusement in the situation. What are the odds? You go up to the other person and say jokingly, "Can I just say you have a fantastic sense of style?" You both laugh, and so do the people around you. It is no longer an awkward situation because you have made light of it. The party attendees respect you for being able to laugh at yourself. Since everyone has seen what a great sense of humor you have, people want to converse and joke around with you for the rest of the night. After a while, no one even thinks about the similar clothes.

The moral of the story is: the only difference between people laughing *at* you and laughing *with* you, is that you're not laughing as well. If you choose to see the humor in your 'embarrassing' moments, you can never be humiliated.

See the absurdity in every situation and always continue to have a good time. Ask yourself, "What difference does this make in the grand scheme of my life?" The answer is likely, "No difference at all."

### 10. Realize there's something to learn from everyone

There's no such thing as truly boring people. Everyone is interesting if you get to know them, and everyone has something to contribute. Magnetic people recognize this. In a new crowd, they stay aware of everyone's unique and positive qualities and they learn from them, when possible. Pay attention to what makes your acquaintances different and use that to hone in what you could learn from them. It could be anything from an effective negotiation strategy or a comedic sensibility to unique stories about a faraway culture or a complex industry you know nothing about. Stay open to learning and allow others to teach you.

### 11. Don't be afraid to say you don't know

When we encounter a topic that we don't understand, many feel the need to pretend to know more than they do. This can suffice for quick encounters when there's not much time to chat, but at all other times, one should never feel ashamed of saying, "That's interesting, I never knew that."

Let's say, you're talking at length with someone and they start bringing up the economy, it's possible that this is a topic you don't know much about. Have the confidence to say, "This sounds fascinating. Tell me more about how it works." You can even use this opportunity to compliment and get to know someone. You could say, "I wish I knew more about this, but I never took time to learn. How did you become so knowledgeable?" We tend to trust people who are open about their shortcomings, as it makes them seem humble, self-aware and comfortable with who they are. It allows us to let our guard down. Furthermore, when we give someone the opportunity to feel like they can teach us something, it makes them feel significant and interesting.

## 12. Do not give any attention to someone who doesn't respect you

We've established that magnetic people are intelligent and empathic, but a necessary quality is also self-respect. You can be kind, complimentary, and try your best to get to know someone, but if they begin behaving rudely, you must drop that social interaction like a hot potato. If you allow someone to disrespect you, then other people will realize they can get away with this behavior. It sends a signal that you have no self-respect and will put up with abuse. Distance yourself from anyone that disrespects you and if you can't, then it's time to brush up on your classy comebacks.

### 13. Build a large network of diverse connections

It can be tempting to only connect or befriend people from your industry of work, but this isn't the way of a magnetic person. Include a diverse range of people in your social circle. Open yourself up to individuals from other cultures, genders, sexual orientations, religions, work industries, and more. Not only can it feel fulfilling to have a large group of friends, but you'll come across as multi-faceted and well-connected.

## All You Need to Know About the Trifecta of Charm

The trifecta of charm consists of intelligence, humor, and empathy. When combined in the right way, this formidable combination of qualities can charm almost anyone. In some cases, it can even override your physical appearance, making you come across as attractive even if you are not conventionally so. While most people embody at least one of these traits, they must work together to produce the best results.

In a conversation, intelligence alone makes one seem stiff and inaccessible, while someone gifted with only humor will come off too childish and silly. Empathy is a valuable trait, but without intelligence or humor it creates an individual that is too soft and overly emotional. The trifecta of charm utilizes all three at once and in equal measure.

Unfortunately, these qualities are also some of the most difficult to teach. In order to develop them, individuals must work hard at assimilating new habits into their personality, and must engage in a significant amount of study. Some trial-and-error may be necessary, and personal style will vary with each person. Still, it is absolutely possible for someone who scores low on all three counts to add the trifecta of charm to their social arsenal. They need only follow these tips:

- **Intelligence**

Intelligence can be described in a number of different ways, but at its core, it's comprised of several basic functions. Problem-solving, reasoning, logic, and critical thinking are some of the most notable. Many believe you're either intelligent or you're not, but this has proven to be far from the truth. Intelligence can always be developed, even in adults. It only requires that people challenge themselves, explore unfamiliar topics and try to assimilate them into their understanding of the world.

You may be wondering why intelligence matters in a conversation. Quite simply, it is easier for intelligent people to connect the dots and expand on any topic that is presented to them. They are sources of interesting information and people tend to like someone they can learn from, as long as the person isn't condescending or hijacking the conversation.

To enhance your intelligence, make sure to:

**1. Expand your mind in a way that you enjoy**

People tend to shy away from this suggestion because they think it means they need to read a heap of books. While reading can definitely expand your mind, there are a variety of other options to better suit your preferences. You can learn about new topics by watching documentaries, educational YouTube videos, television shows, enrolling in a class, taking an online course, or perhaps by asking someone who knows more than you on a certain topic. Information can be transferred in countless ways. You just need to discover what way works best for you.

**2. Discuss a topic with someone who has a different opinion from you**

Learning to have a civil discussion with someone you disagree with is a highly valuable skill. By challenging our perspectives, they force us to reason and think critically, and let's face it, debates can be exciting. Even if you feel strongly that the other person could not be more wrong, it's an excellent exercise for developing your sense of logic. And sometimes we don't realize there's a flaw in our reasoning until we are faced with a challenger. We can learn from their good points as well as their flawed arguments. All we advise is that you keep it civil! Remember, attack the arguments, and not the person making them.

### 3. Practice explaining the new things you've learned

It's no use reading lots of information if we can't actually retain it. One way to ensure you keep all that new data in your head is to try and explain it to someone else. This can be anyone – a partner, a friend, or if you're feeling confident, a new acquaintance.

- **Humor**

To truly enjoy someone's company, there must be some level of humor. It forces us to take it easy, keep it light-hearted, and to see the joy in even the most absurd situations. Without humor, the world would be a miserable place, and this is why it's a vital component of the trifecta. Making someone laugh is an easy way to start developing a connection. In fact, humor is so powerful, it can make people overlook a range of negative qualities.

It's also important to note that having a good sense of humor also requires you to be able to take a joke. If someone pokes fun at you and they don't intend to be mean, try to see the humor in it! Laugh it off and don't be easily offended. And remember, the best kind of humor is not mean or degrading towards another person. Keep it smart and inoffensive.

1. **Immerse yourself in comedic entertainment**

There's no better way to understand the workings of good comedy than by finding comedic entertainment that you enjoy. Watch a funny TV show, movie, stand-up performance, or even YouTube videos. Expose yourself to a variety of comedy styles and choose the one you most enjoy. Try to stay away from comedy that revolves around pranks and slapstick humor. While it's totally fine to enjoy these, one shouldn't expect to learn anything from them.

2. **Practice seeing the absurdity in everyday scenarios**

This skill can be valuable not just for conversation skills but for life in general. It will teach you how to laugh in the face of disasters, and instantly ignite more positivity even on bad days. Laughter is, after all, one of the best remedies for all troubles. Life is filled with absurdity and ridiculousness, you just have to recognize it. The next time you find yourself annoyed by something, try turning it on its head and seeing it as a comedic scenario.

3. **Surround yourself with funny people**

We all know someone with a killer sense of humor, someone who's a joy to be around, and makes us laugh at the drop of a hat. A great way to become funnier or develop a better sense of humor is to spend time with funny people. Listen and laugh at their jokes, try to respond in a similarly lighthearted fashion, and try to learn from the way their humorize certain situations. Notice what they joke about, how they joke about it, and what exactly makes it funny. If there are jokes that fall a little flat, examine why. The best part of this humor-building tactic? You'll enjoy it immensely and spend more time with a friend!

- **Empathy**

Quite simply, empathy is the ability to put yourself in someone else's shoes. It means you can pick up on their emotions, and feel what they're feeling. It's more than just sympathy, empathetic individuals can feel other people's experiences as if they endured them as well.

Most of us are reasonably capable of cognitive empathy, which is when we understand emotion on an intellectual level, but we can't actually relate to what someone is feeling. Sometimes, we may not even really care, but we know what we're supposed to say to be polite. We can recognize that someone is sad, and we know how to act sympathetic, but there's no part of us that feels this person's sadness. We can think about emotions rationally, but all the while, we remain somewhat detached.

Cognitive empathy can prove useful in the workplace and quick everyday conversations, but if you're interested in deep connections, it won't be enough. Thankfully, developing your emotional empathy will also enhance your cognitive empathy, so why not start there?

1. **Become aware of your own emotions and engage in self-love**

It's an uncomfortable truth, but a truth nonetheless; it all begins with you and the way you deal with your emotions. If you're constantly suppressing your feelings and you never deal with them in an honest, healthy way, then it's likely you're unable to relate to the feelings of others. You may find that a part of you resists emotional empathy because it opens a locked box of feelings that you haven't yet dealt with.

2. **Learn the life story of someone you disagree with**

It's easy to empathize with a homeless person or a victim of abuse, but this doesn't prove you're an empathic person – only that you're not a sociopath. To truly build empathy, challenge yourself by delving deeper into the life of someone you disagree with. Try to detach yourself from the opposing view or opinion they hold, and instead try to see them as a unique human being who has led a complex life, no different to you or anyone you're friends with. The goal is not to like them or change your opinion, but instead, to see beyond your perspective and feel someone's experience. It's possible to empathize with someone's problems or issues, and not agree with the choices they made.

This exercise is likely to be more meaningful if it involves someone you know, but if you're not ready for such an encounter, it's possible to use a public figure you don't know personally. This step can be completed in a variety of ways. You can watch the biopic of a historical or famous figure, or if it's someone you know, you can try to get to know them over digital messages or in person. Build the conversation gradually so you don't come across as nosey. Start by asking them about their background or family and lead to questions about their goals or influences. You'd be surprised how much you can relate to someone you don't even like!

3. **Take the time to imagine what being someone else is like**

We've all done this for at least a fleeting second, but rarely do we take the time to do it in depth. Try it. It's an exercise you can do absolutely anywhere, and in any physical position. Choose someone you know reasonably well. Imagine what it was like to have their childhood. Consider what it was like to see their parents every single day. Think of what childhood needs might not have been met. What are this person's insecurities? Imagine what it's like to wake up every morning with those insecurities, and how it plays out in everyday interactions. What kind of situations would bring up those insecurities? Imagine what hardships could have led to those insecurities.

Visualize the experiences this person might have had to result in who they are today. And more than this, consider the privileges you have that this person doesn't. Even if they are wealthier and more successful than you, chances are there are still privileges you have that they don't. Perhaps you have a happier family, perhaps you've never been as unlucky in love, or maybe you have more supportive friends. Imagine what it's like to no longer have those privileges and acknowledge how different your life would be without them.

## Three Steps to Becoming a More Interesting Person

Let's tackle a big question, shall we? Whether we admit it or not, we all want to become a more interesting person. But what does that really mean? Charisma is a major component, but that's not all there is to it. The trifecta of charm can also be considered a dominant influence over how interesting we are, but still, there's a little more to it than that. At the end of the day, being interesting comes with its own attitude – an attitude of openness and eclecticism.

Just think about all the experiences you've had with captivatingly interesting people. It's true that sometimes what's interesting can be subjective, but there are definitely some overarching traits. There tends to be the feeling that the other person is almost a treasure chest of stories and ideas. They have surprises up their sleeve. They know and have seen far more than you. They can't be caught or grasped, cause they are always one step ahead.

Let's use these experiences as a baseline, and figure out how we can emulate them.

1. **Do interesting things**

Doesn't that seem obvious? If you sit at home, watch TV, and stay in your comfortable bubble, you're not going to be very interesting to other people. We all use our experiences as a reference; if you haven't had many varied experiences, you're not going to have all that much to offer to conversations, unless it's with other people who also haven't seen that much. Accumulate fantastic, adventurous, and diverse experiences. Delve into the unknown and push the boundaries of your comfort zone. Do something you never thought you would do and expand your horizons. Collect interesting experiences and you'll become more interesting, in turn.

**2. Think outside of the box**

People are too focused on what they should be doing or saying that they miss the entire point of being interesting. Try thinking outside of the box or turning a situation on its head. This is different to behaving like a rebel or violating social codes; this just means responding in a way that is unusual. For example, if everyone is telling stories about how well-behaved their kid is, make things interesting by telling a story about the funniest thing your kid ever did, even if it was a little bit naughty. If all your friends are wearing modern bikinis, wear a classy high-waisted bikini styled from the 80s. If all your friends are discussing their biggest success at work, instead talk about the biggest failure that you learned the most from. Make situations more interesting by responding differently.

**3. Be open-minded**

No one likes a closed-minded person; the only ones who do are other closed-minded people who are closed-minded about the same things. Stop being so easily offended or shocked and replace those feelings with awe and curiosity. Not only will that make you more absorbent to interesting information, but it will also make you a more interesting conversationalist. The reason we like open-minded people is because they convey a sense of freedom. We actually don't experience closed-minded people as more moral, intelligent, or wise; they come across as caged by their own beliefs. Open-minded individuals can still have strong beliefs, but they are so comfortable and free that they can still listen to alternative opinions. We admire this sense of openness and freedom in others. Instinctively we feel that if a person embodies this attitude, they must have seen a lot and have a lot to share.

Developing all the qualities in this chapter will enhance your conversation skills tenfold. In reality, having better conversations begins with our frame of mind, our social abilities, and the experiences we've had. Work on developing all these skills, and you'll notice conversations coming alive in your presence.

# Chapter 5 - Knowing Your Audience

You may be likable and charming, but no conversation arsenal is complete without the ability to read a room. A conversationalist that can read a room is able to pick up the thoughts, feelings and general personality of every person they observe or engage with. As we mentioned earlier, this skill is paramount to good communication as we need to understand the factors that influence whether our social tactics will succeed or not. The strategies to win over a shy person will likely annoy someone who is very outgoing, and vice versa. Someone who is in a bad mood will not be as receptive to certain social cues as someone who is in a great mood.

## Microexpressions

We think that facial expressions tell us everything but that's not the whole truth. A smile doesn't always indicate happiness, and a serious expression doesn't necessarily indicate nervousness or displeasure. If you want to know how someone is truly feeling, pay attention to their microexpressions.

Microexpressions are nonverbal signals that last anywhere from a fraction of a second to a few seconds – but rarely longer than that. They may be recurring, but if they are permanent, then it's likely the person in question is not trying to hide their feelings at all. Microexpressions occur when we momentarily let our guard down and display our true reaction. Most people have been taught to act polite and always keep a tight rein on their true feelings, and this is why microexpressions are so fleeting. As soon as we feel ourselves slipping, we immediately return to the face we put on for the world.

The emotions we hide are not always negative. We may try to hide our euphoria while we're on a date with a person we really like, or we may try to hide our excitement if we're holding back good news before an official announcement.

Let's consider Rhonda again. While attending a friend's party, she meets a variety of different people with whom she interacts. Since she's not the most socially skilled person, she is met with a range of different reactions.

1. **Stress and impatience**

When Rhonda arrives at the party, she immediately comes across somebody she knows. She stops to talk to her old friend, and unbeknownst to her, she has stopped by a doorway, blocking someone from entering. The stranger stands behind her, clearing his throat, but Rhonda doesn't notice. He purses his lips and his nostrils flare for a moment. When Rhonda eventually takes notice, his jaw tightens before he regains his composure and walks to his intended destination.

2. **Frustration or anger**

While at the party, Rhonda runs into her ex. The relationship ended badly and mostly due to Rhonda's bad behavior. She doesn't recognize him immediately since he cut his hair and started wearing contact lenses. Sitting at a table with some acquaintances, she doesn't realize he is present as well, so she ignores him. The ex is fuming, still bitter about the way she treated him and even more now since she can't recognize him. While he fumes, he presses his lips together and continues to purse them intermittently.

3. **Disdain or dislike**

Rhonda notices two women having a conversation and she joins in. Unfortunately, she changes the topic and begins talking about herself quite incessantly. While Rhonda talks, one woman looks at her askance, only making eye contact with the corner of her eye. She keeps her head tilted away from Rhonda, a sign that she is not enthusiastic about this newcomer's presence and may even feel superior to her. She resists the urge to roll her eyes and in doing so her eyelids flutter with more blinks than usual, sending the message, "The nerve of this woman!"

4. **Disagreement and contempt**

Later on, Rhonda converses with a teacher and makes the argument, "Schools are killing the creativity of children." The teacher disagrees strongly with this, though he still tries to act polite. For a moment, he furrows his brows and asks, "How so?" When furrowed brows accompany narrowed eyes, it indicates disagreement or skepticism, but if the eyes are wide, this signals curiosity. As Rhonda continues, the teacher begins to feel a little contemptuous. One side of his mouth curls up very briefly while the other side remains still. Many people misinterpret this expression as a 'half-smile,' but this is incorrect. This is a classic sign of contempt, especially if the mouth is tight.

### 5. Fear

Someone who had a bad experience with Rhonda at a different party sees her approaching. As she notices Rhonda, her eyes widen for a brief moment, conveying a sense of vigilance. Fear is most easily identified by looking at the eyes. The mouth also reacts by widening horizontally. This is different from a smile where the corners are upturned, when fear is introduced, the corners pull back horizontally towards the ears.

### 6. Excitement or happiness

Even though Rhonda had negative impressions on a lot of people, the person who invited her to the party is happy to see her. Rhonda's friend is in the middle of a serious discussion with someone else, so she's trying to not look too happy, but when she notices Rhonda, her eyes look a bit brighter. Even though she's not smiling, both corners of her mouth turn up very slightly.

# The Six Types of Communicators & How to Win Them Over

Social psychologists have discovered there are six major communication styles. While each of us is more likely to communicate in one of these styles naturally, we can actually learn how to use the talents and traits of all the other styles. For the most part, each type of communicator responds best to those who communicate in the same way, but not all the time. See if you can determine which type you are. And most importantly, figure out how you would approach the other different styles.

- **Noble**

*Straightforward, focused, tells it like it is*

These communicators tend to make great leaders as they have no qualms about saying what needs to be said and participating in the difficult conversations. They are practical, direct, and many people respond well to them since they are always honest. They are not concerned with the feelings of others, preferring to be upfront and straightforward. This doesn't mean they are unfeeling people, they simply don't factor in emotions when they are speaking. Though they usually don't have bad intentions, sensitive people can become upset at what they say since it's often not worded in a considerate manner. They are uncomplicated and usually quite predictable.

## Conversation Skills

To win a Noble communicator over, you must be clear, direct, and confident. Avoid overly flowery language as they don't see the point and will see it as frivolous fluff. Focus on the 'what' and 'how,' since Nobles are most concerned with the practical details than anything else. Give them all the information upfront as they won't chase you for extra details. Other than these general rules, you'll find you can say almost anything to a Noble since they are only concerned with truth and reality.

- **Socratic**

*Expressive, persuasive, intellectual, detailed*

Unlike Noble communicators, Socratic individuals enjoy the long, drawn out discussions with lots of details. These communicators tend to clash with Nobles since their methods of communication are almost completely opposite. It is rare that a Socratic communicator gets into a short chat; as soon as they open their mouth, it's easy for them to get lost in a tangent or a long, flowery anecdote. When they tell stories they add a lot of background information, preferring to present the whole picture. At times, they can seem to be lecturing.

To befriend a Socratic, listen to their long-winded stories with your full attention, and better yet, ask them questions. They enjoy interesting and unique individuals, so make sure to tickle their intellect. Bring up unusual but fascinating topics, and join them as they delve deeply into them with their hundreds of questions and insightful analyses. They prefer to deal with ideas, instead of feelings, though they are more receptive to emotions than Nobles.

- **Reflective**

*Patient, understanding, sensitive, wants to bond*

If you're a reflective communicator, there are likely a lot of people in your life who run to you with their problems. For better or for worse, people enjoy seeking out support from reflectives since they are known for being understanding and having great listening skills. Reflectives like to connect on an emotional basis and usually aren't that interested in sharing strong opinions. It doesn't come naturally to a reflective communicator to be assertive or direct, so they can be dishonest or even deceptive. They would prefer to not see anyone's feelings hurt, so they say what needs to be said to keep conversation harmonious. Reflectives are the most likely communicators to get interrupted or overlooked in conversation, since they usually don't express themselves in a strong or confident manner.

To win a Reflective over, open up a little and show some vulnerability. Find common ground with them and share your mutual passions or interests. To really capture a Reflective's attention, ask them questions and encourage them to open up to you as well. They are so used to listening to other people and letting someone else take the spotlight that they can feel overlooked. Give them some kind attention and you'll win them over, for sure.

- **Candidate**

## Conversation Skills

*Pleasant, talkative, analytical, wants to be liked*

When we combine the Socratic and Reflective styles, we get the Candidate communicator. Candidates are warm, chatty, and usually have a pleasant air about them. They enjoy connecting with others by telling stories, and will always make the effort to keep conversation harmonious. When a problem arises, they believe that talking is the best solution, and they do so in an emotionally engaged manner. They are more truthful than someone with only a Reflective style, but they still try their best to avoid messy conflict.

To get on their good side, turn on your good listening skills and be patient while they talk. If you stop paying attention or end a conversation abruptly, the Candidate will likely feel very annoyed. Since they also have Reflective attributes, they are a lot more receptive to other points of view than a Socratic communicator alone. Win them over by really engaging with them, sharing genuine parts of yourself, and listening closely to their long, sometimes emotional, stories.

- **Magistrate**

*Intense, argumentative, persuasive*

The Noble and Socratic styles fuse together to create the big presence of the Magistrate. These individuals can be incredibly eloquent and persuasive, but while they excel as public speakers, they can be a little slow in their interpersonal relationships. It takes them longer to grasp individual needs and sensitivities, so they can sometimes act out of line and offend people closest to them. When we witness a Magistrate communicator speaking, it can seem like they'd make a phenomenal leader. Oftentimes, it can come across like a monologue or a grand speech. Unfortunately, Magistrates tend to divide audiences and at their worst, can be preachy and overbearing. You either love them or you hate them. In their personal lives, they can be argumentative, and they may even get into trouble at work.

To get close to a Magistrate, be unafraid of serious, deep discussions. They don't shy away from the dark topics that, they feel, convey the real truth of life. It's also necessary that you understand how to speak calmly and rationally in heated discussions without flying off the handle. Otherwise you may find yourself in a full-blown argument with a Magistrate. Also make sure to listen closely to the Magistrate as they feel strongly that what they're saying needs to be heard. To flatter them, make them feel like the revolutionary they think they are.

- **Senator**

*Strategic, adaptable, observant, versatile*

The most complex of the six, the Senator is often considered the most clever communication style. In conversation, the way they speak and the things they say are all carefully calculated to produce the outcome they desire. They have the unique ability to combine the skills of the other five styles to create a predetermined effect. They may speak like a Noble, but also have the listening skills of a Reflective. They are highly unpredictable, and many people who try to get to know them may perceive them as fickle.

Trying to coax a Senator into your corner is no easy task. Of the six communicators, they are definitely the most difficult to catch. This is because they are always changing, and often their behavior is determined by what they hope to achieve. This is not always a selfish pursuit, sometimes the goal can be to help other people get along. The exact goal depends on the individual personality. We advise observing Senators closely and paying attention to the transitions between communication styles. One can often identify what their goal is by noticing what method of communication they are using at that moment. Reflect whichever style they appear to be using.

## Conversation Tips for Special Audiences

As we've demonstrated, conversation tactics are not the same for everyone. And even though we've covered a wide range of personality types already, there are a few others we still haven't accounted for.

### Children

It shouldn't be so scary to talk to tiny humans, but many people don't have experience with children. If you have to meet a new partner's kid or bond with a younger cousin, it will not serve you well to be filled with anxiety – though it wouldn't be completely unfounded.

After all, children can't talk about the same topics as adults. And what if you accidentally say something that scares them?

The reality is, it's not as difficult as you think, and children are a lot smarter than people give them credit for. Children tend to respond positively when adults lower themselves to their height. When you're not a looming giant, you're more approachable. When you speak, make sure to use positive language. Instead of just saying, "Your mom has told me a lot about you" try sweetening it up by saying "Your mom has told me so much about how talented and smart you are!" Remember that kids love the idea of adventure, so if you're going to tell them any stories, make sure it has a hint of adventure. And ask them questions about what they enjoy. Kids will warm up to you when they can talk about whatever excites them.

When you talk to a kid, fully embrace silliness and you'll definitely get on their good side. And remember, do not ever correct a child when they are speaking playfully! If they said they visited the land of unicorns, do not say "Unicorns don't exist." Instead, ask them what it's like there and if they made any unicorn friends.

**The Elderly**

It's no secret that as people get older, they become less physically and mentally capable of behaving as they used to. One common mistake people make, however, is talking to them like they're children. While they may be a little slower, you'll find that most elderly individuals are still incredibly sharp, especially when you ask them about the passions of their life. Shoot them a few questions about how they met their life partner, the career they had, or where they came from, and you'll find that they suddenly regain all their wits (provided none of these questions trigger something traumatic!) and enjoy sharing the fascinating stories they hold. Bear with them if their memory slows down, and allow them to find their thoughts.

Always speak to the elderly like the adults they are. Dumbing down your speech is not only rude, but it can actually do harm to their mental processes. Why? For the same reason you'd suffer if someone dumbed down their speech towards *you*. It lowers their self-esteem and quickens the decline of their cognitive abilities because no one is allowing them to use their mind properly.

There are as many communication styles as there are human beings in the world. No two people communicate in the exact same way – but this guide will help you navigate the major personalities. To identify what their exact style is like, consider their age, background, culture, interests, and their general nature. Everything is a clue; pay attention.

# Chapter 6 - Building Deep Connections

At the end of the day, we all crave something beyond lighthearted banter or party discussions. We want to bond with others. We want to see our humanity mirrored in another person, and we want to mirror theirs. Many will even argue that this is what life is all about – learning to live in harmony with others so we can help each other excel. Whatever you believe, it stands true for everyone: we all need deep connections. Without them, we can even become more susceptible to mental illness.

Since we all need it to thrive, you'd think it would be easy to make lasting and deep connections. But for the majority of us, they are few and far between. Often the most meaningful connections we have are with people we've known for a long time.

There are many reasons we may find this feat difficult. Sometimes it's because we're afraid of intimacy. Sometimes it's because we can be judgmental, and we want to believe there's nothing we could possibly have in common with the people around us. And of course many times, we just don't have the necessary social skills. We want a meaningful connection, but we just don't know how to get from A to B.

Here's some good news: it's actually not as difficult as you think.

## Conversation Tricks to Instantly Build Rapport with Someone

### 1. Try to reflect their speaking style

Pay attention to the rhythm, length, and word choices with which someone speaks. To build rapport, try and mirror their style of speech. If there are words they use often, work them into your side of the dialogue as well. It's important, when doing this, to not copy them entirely, or they'll feel like you're making fun of them. To avoid this, a good rule of thumb is to never mimic someone's accent.

### 2. Seek out their advice

Instead of asking for someone's opinion, ask for their advice. Doing this will strengthen your bond. Why? For starters, you come across as being genuine (only honest people can admit they need advice!) and second of all, you're showing them you think they're a credible source of feedback. After this interaction, they are also likely to feel invested in the issue they advised you on and they may want to keep up with what happens. Just make sure you pay close attention to them and listen to what they're saying carefully.

### 3. Combine ideas

You don't have to be at a work meetup to brainstorm; you can do this with anyone. All it involves is playing off their ideas and expanding on them. When you brainstorm with someone, whether casually or seriously, you show them you've been paying close attention to them and that you take their ideas seriously. In addition to this, you may satisfy their need for expansion, by showing that you have something to offer them intellectually.

## 4. Paraphrasing

When we paraphrase what someone says, we repeat what they said in our own words. The paraphrase should always be combined with another statement such as "I understand." Or, it can be turned into a question with the addition of something to the effect of "Is that right?" Paraphrasing shows that you've listened, understood, and empathized with what they've said. For example, if your friend says, "I'm an insomniac so please excuse me if I seem a little out of it," you could say, "I understand. You didn't get enough sleep, so of course you feel exhausted and disoriented." By saying this, you're not adding any new information, only rephrasing the previous statement slightly.

## 5. Ask questions that involve 'how' and 'why'

If you're not sure what kind of questions to ask, think of something that begins with 'how' or 'why.' These types of questions create bonds because you're asking your conversation partner to search themselves for more elaborate and meaningful answers. For example, if your friend is talking about a high-pressure meeting she just finished. You could ask "How do you feel about it now?" or "Why do you think it went so well?"

Building rapport is essential to creating a bond with empathy and connection, but we won't get there immediately. It involves a lot more than conversation tactics.

## How to Form Meaningful Relationships

### 1. Let people in

All the other points on this list mean nothing if you don't let people in. Don't act cold and aloof as this forms a barrier between yourself and others. Instead, try to exude an inviting aura and allow them to get to know you, as much as you get to know them. People often make the mistake of feeling like a victim when other people don't take an interest in getting to know them. Do not fall into this victim complex. Instead, ask yourself: am I showing this person that I can be trusted? Am I allowing people to get close to me? Am I showing them what makes me a good friend?

### 2. Balance giving and taking

If your friend bought you lunch at your last hang-out, buy them a drink or meal at your next hang-out. Return generosity with generosity. If you aren't in a good place financially, offer to do something else for them. There is beauty in having a friend or family member that would do anything for us, but our responsibility as a good person is to never ask them to do *everything* for us. If you come to the realization that you've been talking about your problems non-stop for the last hour, take the time to ask your close connection how they are, and make sure to offer them the same patience. Always be aware of when you might be asking for too much. And if you must, then ensure you make it up to them.

It's also important to note that the reverse should also be avoided. If your friend continuously asks you for a lot, be honest about how you feel and create some boundaries.

### 3. Make time to maintain the bond

Once we form a bond with a new friend or partner, we need to make the effort to nurture this relationship. It doesn't matter how well we get along with someone else – if we never make time for them in our lives, this bond will slowly dissipate. And when a reconnection is made in the distant future, it'll feel like you're starting all over again.

The act of making time is a powerful one, and it sends an important message: I care enough about you to always find time for you. If one party embarks on a long travel experience, or moves to a different city, make the effort to do a weekly or fortnightly catch-up session on the phone. Avoid having a dynamic where you only speak when one person needs a shoulder to cry on. Even partners that live together must find time in their busy schedules to maintain the bond. Creating quality time is a necessary part of keeping a connection alive.

### 4. Eradicate all competitive behavior

When we're close to someone, it's easy to start comparing ourselves to them. If your friend or partner is further along in their career than you are, never allow feelings of envy to drive your actions. It's perfectly normal for a jealous thought to cross your brain, but never let it trigger a decision that affects them. It's totally fine to think, "Gee, Adam is really having an affect on all the girls at this party. I wish I could do that." But it is not okay to start telling someone about his most embarrassing moment just to take him down a peg. Recognize that you both have different strengths and weaknesses, and that life is not a competition. Look for inspiration in your relationships, not competition.

**5. Know the purpose your relationship serves**

Each person in our life helps us in a slightly different way. Recognizing the greater purpose they serve can ignite feelings of appreciation and will ultimately help us strengthen the bond. The gifts they bring to our lives are far more specific than just giving us emotional support or preventing us from feeling bored. If you think about it, each person we know provides us with a unique lesson. See if you can identify the people who continuously teach you these lessons – and work out which ones you teach other people.

- Embrace everything that makes you different.
- It's okay to cry and talk about your feelings.
- Opposites attract and help each other grow.
- Everything can be fun if you let it be.
- The world is full of amazing experiences and you need to chase them all.

- We must always face ourselves exactly as we are and strive to be better.
- Just enjoy things as they are, there's no need to make it complicated.
- A true friend is with you during your darkest hours.

## The Habits of Emotionally Intelligent People

Remember when we discussed how magnetic individuals are adept at emotional self-sufficiency? That's a major attribute of emotional intelligence. An emotionally intelligent individual can not only sense, understand, and empathize with the feelings of others, they also have a firm grasp on their own emotions.

Believe it or not, emotional intelligence is a bigger indicator of one's success than their IQ. While an IQ is more likely to earn you a particular job, your level of emotional intelligence will determine whether you keep that job, or whether you get promoted. More than this, however, emotional intelligence is vital for fulfilling personal relationships, whether it's with family, friends, or romantic partners. Some people are born with an intrinsic gift for emotional intelligence, but it's completely possible for others to learn and develop the skill over time. Let's examine the life-altering habits of emotionally intelligent people.

- **They always find common ground**

## Conversation Skills

When in conversation with someone, emotionally intelligent people focus on the similarities instead of the potential conflicts. It doesn't matter who it is or how different that person seems to be, they always converse with the intention of finding common interests and values. Even if the person they're talking to openly disagrees with them about something, individuals with a high EQ choose to focus on the similarities. When faced with conflict, they have the maturity to say, "Let's agree to disagree."

- **They are self-aware**

Self-awareness is a key attribute of emotional intelligence. This means that an individual has a good understanding of who they are, how they feel, what their triggers are, and how they are most likely to react in a given scenario.

Let's take Sally, for instance. She's has an extremely high EQ. After a bad day at work, she recognizes that she's feeling anxious and sad. Her friends invite her to have dinner at the mall. She knows that when she's sad, she is more likely to shop and overspend, so she has the self-awareness to realize that being near a shopping mall is not a good idea.

- **They are masters of self-discipline and self-management**

Remember when Sally recognized that going to the mall on a bad day would have a terrible outcome? Awareness is one thing, but having the discipline to say no is another. Self-awareness and self-discipline go together like bread and butter. After all, what's the point of being aware of the best course of action if you can't bring yourself to actually take that action?

Emotionally intelligent people are not slaves to their impulses. They are not prone to big bursts of anger or indignation; they deal with their feelings privately and if something must be done, they go about it maturely. They have the strength of mind to suppress behavior that will only cause damage and destruction, even if it causes momentary agitation. They don't expect other people to take care of their feelings, instead they take care of themselves.

- **They are always aware of subtext**

Everyone knows there's a big difference between the words people speak and what they're *actually* saying. High EQ individuals are always aware of this subtext. They are masters at interpreting tones of voice, word pacing, and the general vibe given off by each person they meet. With everything that they gage through observation, they are able to understand what's not being said. Intuition and 'gut feelings' can also help with deciphering subtext. If you get a strong feeling about something, chances are you're onto some subtext.

- **They steer clear from blame games**

Emotionally intelligent people are masters of accountability and acceptance. When something goes wrong, they resist the urge to point the finger elsewhere. They recognize that it usually takes more than one person to create a certain situation. If we find out a friend talked about us behind our back, it's easy to put all the blame on them and say they shouldn't have been doing that. But what if your friend was saying she's angry because you owe her a lot of money and she doesn't think you'll ever pay her back? It's important that we recognize our part in every situation. It's not about feeling guilty, it's about admitting that we have more power than we realize and owning up to the repercussions.

It's true that sometimes we can fault one person for something that goes wrong. If you took all safety precautions and someone robbed you anyway, it seems very clear who should be blamed. Not you, but them. Avoiding the blame game doesn't mean you can never say that someone else made a mistake; it means that you don't get stuck in a loop of blame where you cause yourself to suffer more than you need to. It's the difference between thinking "That man made a mistake" and "What an awful man. How dare he? Now everything is ruined and it's all because of him."

## Why Self-Compassion is Important for Healthy Relationships

A well-known misconception about fulfilling relationships is the idea that we need to give, give, and give to our closest companions. Kindness and empathy towards others are important parts of every relationship, that's true, but it's imperative that we never neglect our own needs. In fact, a good rule of thumb is to treat yourself the way you would treat a good friend. We would never ask a friend to give until she has nothing, and so we should never ask that of ourselves.

## Conversation Skills

Self-compassion helps us recharge so we can continue to do our best for the world we live in. When we drain ourselves of energy, we are more prone to depression, moodiness, or general exhaustion. We drain ourselves of everything we need to continue being a good friend. Indirectly, self-compassion helps the people we care about as well.

Here are the ways in which we can show ourselves self-compassion in our everyday relationships:

- Your friends want you to stay out late for a big night out, but you're exhausted from work and don't really want to go. Instead of forcing yourself to go out because everyone wants you to, put self-care first. Tell your friends: "I'm going to take a raincheck and stay home to rest. I'm extremely tired, so I know you understand. Let's do something else soon!"
- You're with a group of people who are all sharing raunchy sex stories. You've always been a more private person and you start to feel uncomfortable with the topic. When everyone looks at you expectantly, waiting for a story, don't feel pressured. Just say: "I'd prefer to keep this part of my life private, so I'm going to pass." Or if you're with a closer group of friends, feel free to tell them, "I'm not really comfortable sharing such intimate stories. Could we change the topic?"
- You run into a friend that you aren't very close to. She hears you broke up with your partner and is pressuring to tell you

## Conversation Skills

everything that happened, even though you don't want to talk about it. Be kind to yourself, and don't give in to pressure if it causes you distress. Tell her: "I'm not ready to talk about it yet. It's still hard to think about, so I'll have to tell you another time. Thanks for your concern."

- If a family member said something extremely hurtful and they suddenly want to see you, be compassionate towards yourself and ask yourself if you're ready or if you even want to. When someone hurts us it can take a while before we feel safe around them again. This is not our fault, and we should always make sure we are ready for future interactions.

Healthy and deep relationships require both parties to be taken care of. To develop more fulfilling connections, make sure both sides get what they need every time – and yes, that means you too! Make sure boundaries are respected and balance is always attained.

# Chapter 7 - Difficult Situations & Social Blunders

It's bound to happen at some point. Unfortunately, it's usually when you least expect it. You think everything is going swimmingly and feel like you're as smooth as honey, but then the unexpected happens. Perhaps you say something you shouldn't have – an easy flub or a major no-no – or perhaps the circumstances are out of your control, and a real jerk comes out of nowhere, derailing all your well-played moves and making you look like a fool.

We're not perfect and neither is anyone else. Awkward moments *will* happen and some of them will be mind-numbingly cringeworthy. In addition to this, rude people are aplenty, and we're going to encounter them whether we like it or not. To become a master of conversation, it's necessary that you understand how to diffuse a difficult social situation. There may be rocky roads ahead, so it's best to gear up.

## How to talk your way out of difficult or awkward situations

Don't just sit back and go red in the face. There are many ways we can use speech and conversation to mitigate a difficult conversation.

You'd be surprised by how much we can accomplish with these quick tips.

- **You offended someone**

There are many reasons you could find yourself in this difficult position. You might have encountered someone who was easy to offend, or maybe, just maybe, you said something legitimately terrible. The first step is always to apologize, whether you mean it or not, and let them know you didn't mean to offend them. The second step is up to you.

**i)** Insist you chose your words wrongly and that it wasn't what you meant to say. If you can, amend what you said with better, less offensive phrasing. You can also chalk it down to a lack of sleep or fatigue, and tell them you're not as articulate as you normally are.

**ii)** Take the fall, be vulnerable and shift power from you to the other party. For example, let's say you accidentally insulted the way your friend dressed for a party and she is noticeably upset. Clear things up immediately by saying, "I'm sorry. Actually it's me, not you. I'm feeling very self-conscious in this outfit, and you look great. I'm a little jealous, so I projected how I feel about myself onto you."

- **Someone openly insults you**

Awful, shocking, humiliating; these are some of the words you could use to describe the moment when someone insults you. It may be direct and outright, or heavily implied. Either way, it will likely shake you to your core.

The first step is to consider whether we were truly insulted. Oftentimes, we can perceive brutally honest statements as insulting, but really they are just based on a harsh truth we don't want to accept. If we find the insult is more factual than not, then accept what's being said, apologize if necessary, and adjust your behavior, taking into account this new feedback.

You may also figure out the insult was real, and that a person really did just attack your character. In that case, you may follow any of these steps:

**i)** Use humor to undermine and ridicule the insult. This one takes some skill but when done correctly, you can win over an entire audience.

**ii)** Stand up for yourself in an honest and calm way. This does not mean fighting back. If someone calls you an idiot for not knowing something, you can respond by saying, "I'm not an idiot. No one knows everything and we're all learning here." By defending yourself in a mature manner, you'll bound to come out of the situation on-top.

**iii)** Let it slide but bring it up in private, afterwards. If you're not quick on your feet, it's okay to say nothing or laugh it off for the time being. Later on, you can take the person aside and confront them about what they said. This option is more likely to get a meaningful reaction from the person who insulted you. After the heat of the moment, people often regret their mistakes. Be honest about how uncalled for and hurtful it was to be insulted. This direct confrontation may make this person apologize.

- **Someone tries to argue with you**

When we get into a conversation, most people make the effort to keep it harmonious. For many reasons, however, you may encounter someone with an argumentative approach. This can be because they feel passionately against something you said, or it may be down to their personality. Assuming you have no interest in entering this argument, you can follow any of these steps:

**i)** Say "Let's agree to disagree." Completely disengage from the heated discussion. Cut it off before it gets worse.

**ii)** Listen to the other person's point of view. At the end of the day, the person just wants you to see their side. Allow them to fill you in, all the while saying that you see their point. Acknowledge that they have interesting points, but avoid mentioning your opinion. Turning on your listening skills is another effective way to avoid an argument.

- **Someone hits on you obnoxiously and can't take a hint**

Women experience this more often than men. You could be anywhere, on a bus or at a party, and someone may decide to make a move. Through body language and the nature of your speech, you get across that you're not interested, but the flirty individual does not budge.

**i)** Tell them to stop. Sometimes it can feel like this is the worst thing you can do, but it's usually the most effective method. The other person can't take a hint so sometimes there is no other way but to tell them outright. It doesn't have to be rude if you're trying to let this person off gently. You could say, "You're making me feel uncomfortable. I'm really not interested. I have been trying to let you know discreetly, but perhaps I'm not being clear enough."

**ii)** Mention that you have a partner. In conversation, let slip that you have a boyfriend or girlfriend, or a husband or wife. If you can gush about them, the more likely they'll leave you alone. You can even do this if you don't have a partner; just be prepared to answer questions, if they ask.

**iii)** Seek out the company of a third person. If you're at a social gathering, ask someone else to join you or excuse yourself to join a different conversation. Don't be afraid to quietly tell another person (ideally of the same gender as you) that you need some help getting rid of an obnoxious flirt. Most people will sympathize with you and try to help.

- **You need to break up with a boyfriend or fire an employee**

These are some of the most difficult conversations to start. And yet, mastering how to do it can make a genuine difference in the rejected

## Conversation Skills

person's life. A bad rejection or relationship end can either lower someone's self-esteem, or empower them to grow. To ensure it's the latter instead of the former. Follow these tips.

**i)** Make the time and do it in person. Even though the situation is extremely uncomfortable for you, no doubt, don't rush through the talk and make the meeting as personal as possible. It's harder for the other person than it is for you, so make sure to allow them all the closure they need. If they don't get closure, there's a higher chance they'll take it badly and find it difficult to move on.

**ii)** Tell them the issues honestly, but also mention their potential. We should always be fairly honest about what's not working out. If you're breaking up with your partner because you feel like you're not compatible, it's okay to tell them that. But make sure to also mention something that will not make them feel like a failure. Empower them to find another partner or employer. If you're parting with them because of an existing problem, give them constructive advice for how to grow. Also be prepared for the possibility they will give you feedback as well.

**iii)** End the conversation on a positive note. It may be a sad and awkward occasion, but there's no reason it has to end on that note. Wish them good luck in all their future endeavours. Tell them you're so sure they'll find a job or partner that's right for them, very soon!

## Coping with Difficult Personalities

It doesn't matter how many social tactics you have up your sleeve; when a difficult person comes into play, sometimes they can be intent on ruining the mood or heating up a conversation. For a number of difficult people, it is just the way they are, but it's important to note that for the majority of people, it could just be a bad day or a rough period in their life. While this doesn't excuse their behavior, it should encourage us to empathize with them and resist the urge to be nasty.

Before we discuss the specific types of difficult personalities, here are three general rules to keep in mind:

- Consider what their real need is. What is it they really want that they don't know how to get in a healthy way? There can be general needs that are common to certain personality types, but often they can be specific to the individual.

- Stay calm and listen to what they're saying before you respond.

- Take the high road and continue to treat them with respect.

**1. The Egomaniac**

Egomaniacs have an inflated sense of self-importance and somehow conversation always seems to lead back to how great they are. They can be overt egomaniacs, talking shamelessly about their accomplishments, but sometimes it can be subtle. Many attempt to seem like a normal person, but you'll find they don't really care about what you're saying, and if they do, they may display some competitiveness. To spot an egomaniac, look out for someone with extreme confidence. They will likely carry a sense of entitlement which manifests in an attitude of "This is so unfair!" over something minor. Egomaniacs are usually alone, but if they're not, they are accompanied by other egomaniacs or a very submissive partner.

*The real need*: Most times, what can appear as egomania is actually a deep insecurity and weak emotional foundation. Deep down inside, they feel there is something lacking so they must overpower this gut instinct by shouting about how great they are. If they don't do this, they will have to face their true feelings about themselves, and they are so weak, they cannot handle this reality. What they really need is recognition – but not about their surface accomplishments. Instead they need assurance about their deeper qualities. They have so much insecurity about their real self, that they overcompensate and show-off with the other aspects of their life they can control, such as what car they drive, who they've slept with, or how much money they make.

Sometimes, however, the egomaniac you've met is a sociopath. They do not feel remorse or empathy, and they can be extremely smart. These people do not crave recognition, and their need is simply to dominate others.

*Solution:* An egomaniac cannot take criticism well and is not capable of accountability, so you'd be wasting your time trying to get an apology. The best way to deal with them is to not take what they say seriously and avoid giving them the flattery that they desire. In discussions, only deal in facts and never emotions. Remember, they do not care about your emotions, only their own.

**2. The Bully**

No one likes a bully and if you encounter one, it's likely you're not the only person trying to fight him off. The bully enjoys shaming, humiliating, or singling out the people around him. He gets a noticeable thrill from catching someone off guard or seeing them speechless after he belittles them. Most of the time, a bully only acts this way when he's in group settings. One-on-one, you may find him to be quite insecure and standoffish, but not always. Adult bullies can cause just as much damage as child bullies, but unfortunately, they aren't confronted on their behavior as much; adults do not like admitting that they are dealing with a bully.

*The real need*: Bullies usually come from home lives where they were overpowered or bullied themselves. Their behavior is rooted in a feeling of having no control or power; this is why they seek out scenarios where they can feel powerful. Even if it's not rooted in a traumatic home life, the need of all bullies is similar: to feel powerful and superior by stirring someone's emotions and making them feel inferior.

## Conversation Skills

*Solution:* Bullies enjoy inciting a reaction in their target, so whatever you do, act calm and avoid being reactive. Remain cool in the face of their aggression and they'll soon realize they can't get what they want from you. Realize that they are behaving from an immature, childlike need, so you must treat it as such. Do not give them the pleasure of feeling like they hold sway over your emotions. If you know this bully well, call them out on their behavior and do not let them get away with it.

### 3. The Victim

Make no mistake, the victim may look like a harmless, pathetic individual, but they can do a lot of damage, even without their realizing it. Victims always feel persecuted, like they're constantly getting the short end of the stick. They may accuse others of treating them differently or behaving cruelly towards them, even if no such thing occurred. These people love to talk about their personal problems. They are prone to oversharing and can do so for extended periods of time. If you try to bring up your own problems, they will respond with an attitude that says, "My problem is much worse." If a Victim causes harm to another individual, they have a hard time holding themselves accountable. They believe they cannot hurt others, since they are the real ones hurting.

*The real need*: At some point in the Victim's life, they did not get the empathy or sympathy they needed from an important person, such as a parent. During some life event, they were truly the victim in the situation but no one recognized this. Because they didn't get the closure they needed, they continued to carry this need for sympathy into the other areas of their life. The Victims are in need of empathy, but more than anything, they also need boundaries. They need to realize what happened to them in the past is separate from what's happening now.

*Solution:* To sidestep all the drama of the Victim, do not play into their hands. Once you get them started on their troubles, it's hard for them to stop. Instead, deal with them positively and give them the opposite of what they want to hear. Say things like, "I'm sorry to hear that, but it's great that at least you had wonderful friends to help you!" Even if they are not convinced by your positivity, it will show them they cannot drag you down into their self-pitying hole. If you know the person well, give them boundaries. For example, say you'll listen to them complain for five to ten minutes, but after that, you are only interested in discussing solutions to the problems.

### 4. The Negative Nancies

Like Victims, negative individuals can come across as nice people. Once you get into a more in depth conversation, however, you'll notice one thing: they exude so much negativity! They are distrustful and always see the downside of every issue. They will discourage you from the slightest risk, and you may leave interactions with them feeling more worried, and a lot less excited.

*The real need*: In the negative person's eyes, they are not being negative, only realistic. By being negative, they are attempting to gain control over the situation by staying aware of the worst case scenario. At some point in the past, they let their guard down and something bad happened that was out of their control. Ever since then, they've needed to feel like they have control, so they always expect the worst case scenario. Unfortunately, by doing this, it tends to become a self-fulfilling prophecy.

*Solution:* Counter their negativity with positivity, but remember that it's not your responsibility to make them happy. Show the Negative Nancy that they do have control over creating a positive outcome. And show them that infusing negativity into every situation can actually bring about a negative outcome. Consider sharing some interesting stories from your life where you took a risk and it resulted in something highly positive.

### 5. The Contrarians

It's normal to have a dose of contrarianism in us, but true contrarians take it to an extreme. It doesn't matter what you say, even if it's completely reasonable, the contrarian will always take the opposing side. They love to debate and don't really care what people think about them. Oftentimes, they'll even play Devil's advocate, taking on an unpopular opinion, just to spark a good argument. Anyone who loves debating may get along with a contrarian, but even then, the constant challenge can get exhausting.

*The real need*: The needs of contrarians can vary. Sometimes the individual really wants to come across as a unique person – someone who stands out of the crowd. Other times it can come from a genuine distrust of authority; so whatever the leading opinion is, they immediately expect something suspicious behind it. When they stand up against a perceived authority, it is a rebellion and an attempt to feel superior. Sometimes they feel they are doing the right thing, but other times it is purely to satisfy their own ego. If they can own you in an argument, then in their mind, they have asserted their superiority over some authority force.

*Solution:* Contrarians are some of the most likely personalities to start arguments. The best way to avoid it is to focus on finding common ground with them. Since they are so passionate about certain issues, a "let's agree to disagree" approach may not always work. In this case, try to take a listening approach. Instead of arguing, question them about their opinions and get them to explain it to you further. It cannot become an argument if you don't insert your opinion into the matter.

If you do argue with a contrarian, stick to the facts. Do not get noticeably frustrated or overcome with emotion as some contrarians enjoy this. Another way to avoid a debate is to get the contrarian to tell you their opinion first. That way you'll know how to agree with them and prevent an argument.

## When is it okay to lie?

We're all told that lying is bad, but it's not always that simple. We should never lie to manipulate or mislead, but there are many occasions where lying may be helpful or beneficial. If you're not sure whether it's okay to lie in a particular situation, ask yourself these questions. The more times you answer 'yes,' the more likely it is that you *shouldn't lie.*

- If I lie, will I prolong a situation that's harmful to someone?

- If I lie, am I enabling someone's unhealthy delusion?

- If I lie, will I save myself from potential danger?

- If I tell the truth, will I lower their self-esteem?

- If I tell the truth, will I hurt someone's feelings over something they have no control of?

# Chapter 8 - Using Conversation to Get What You Want

The best conversationalists are constantly using words to wield their way. It can be something as minor as convincing a friend to come out with you or as major as convincing your boss you need a massive raise. And if you're not doing it, chances are it's been done to you. The craziest part is you're not going to even be aware of the most successful ploys against you. The most persuasive conversationalists can slip by unnoticed like a black cat in the dark.

As we've demonstrated, it's never just about what you say, it's also largely about how you behave. Your behavior will set the stage for your words, and will strongly influence how they come across. That's why, in the arena of persuasion, we must also begin with behavioral tactics.

## Subtle ways of showing dominance

Showing real dominance is not just about being a jerk or acting cocky. In fact, if you're coming across as a nasty person, you're just displaying aggressive behavior. This takes no skill and it's not a sustainable method of taking or maintaining power. You're playing on everyone's need to defend themselves against violence by cornering them, and making them feel they have no other choice. True dominance, on the other hand, is achieved by getting others to follow your lead willingly.

If two people, equal in experience and skill, are interviewed for the same job, dominant behavior can make one party appear more competent. Why? It's about far more than what you see on paper. A person who displays dominant behavior shows potential leadership abilities and the big winner, confidence. It presents the illusion that their competence is stronger than the other person, even if it may not be true. Even outside of the professional arena, dominant behavior makes it more likely for people to listen to you and it increases your level of attractiveness to the opposite sex.

That said, you don't need to become a total alpha to succeed, you just need to keep some of these tips in mind for when the right scenario reveals itself.

### 1. Make your body bigger

The psychology behind this sign of dominance has its roots in our animalistic natures. In the animal kingdom, many beasts display the largeness of their size in order to intimidate the other contenders. The one that appears biggest wins by default, without the need to incite violence. Humans can also do this to successfully assert their dominance. To make your body look big, open out your chest, stand tall, and if it doesn't look unnatural, put your hands on your hips. In addition to the above, women can also show dominance by wearing high heeled shoes.

### 2. Walk through the middle of the room

When in a crowded room, people have a tendency to make their body smaller and move through whatever side of the room has the most space. Instead of adjusting to the room, try making the room adjust to you. Walk through the middle of the room, even if there's a crowd, and expect people to move out of the way for you. Most people want to avoid bumping into someone, so they'll budge if you refuse to.

### 3. Sit at the head of the table

The person who sits at the head of the table oversees everything. They can keep a watchful eye on anyone, and they occupy the only seat that does not share its level with someone else. The next time you're with a group, sit in that dominant seat.

## Conversation Skills

### 4. Use hand gestures and touch

To assert dominance, make good use of your hands. Make sure to initiate handshakes by extending your hand first. Then remember, to shake firmly. While you're talking, use your hands expressively, but keep your wrists strong and never limp. Dominant individuals also touch other people, even if they don't know them very well. This is not sexual. This can be a friendly knock on the shoulder, a slap on the knee, or perhaps even a hand placed on their back followed by a directive statement like, "Let's get you another drink."

### 5. Speak with a louder voice

Studies have shown that the loudest voice in the group is seen as the most dominant. Even if they speak less than others, it will make all others pause due to its volume alone. Use your lungs and diaphragm to achieve a louder voice. As you attempt this, do not yell or shout while you're in conversation, as this will only alarm and possibly scare away the people around you.

It is also extremely important to ensure that your voice never gets higher in pitch when you converse. When we are in the presence of someone we feel is superior, our voices immediately get higher pitched than usual. Keep your voice at its normal pitch at all times to avoid coming across as submissive.

Now that we've got our behavior under control, let's get a back-and-forth going.

## Persuasion Techniques for all Situations

### 1. Framing

When it comes to swaying people in a direction of your choice, the art of framing is a classic. When we frame something, we highlight whichever attributes will help our argument best, while paying less attention or even hiding its less appealing factors.

Let's say you're trying to convince a friend of yours to go on holiday with you and your family. To help your argument, you should mention the beautiful location, the fun activities, the luxurious hotel rooms, the attractive locals, etc. And you should avoid talking at length about your annoying Aunt Margaret and the fact that it'll be crowded during the tourist season. If your friend already suspects the risks, then acknowledge them, but emphasize the aspects that will help your argument.

**2. The yes ladder**

This psychological technique has proven successful at eliciting a 'yes' response when used correctly. The first step is to think of the big question you need a positive response to. Once you've determined what this is, start thinking of smaller, relevant asks that are more likely to get a 'yes' response. Gradually work your way through the easy asks, before ending with the big question.

For example, let's say you're trying to convince your family to go on holiday, but you know they're hesitant to leave their normal routine. You would start off with questions like, "Do you ever feel like there's so much in the world you haven't seen yet?" and "Do you agree that life is most fulfilling when you're taking risks and experiencing something new?" You could even throw in, "Do you ever feel like you're wasting your life playing it too safe?" Chances are they will say yes to all these questions. Once you've extracted all the 'yes' answers, your big ask has a much higher chance of success. Finally, you ask, "Perhaps it's time, then, to go on holiday and finally have some new experiences?"

**3. The unreasonable request**

If the yes ladder isn't quite your approach, then why not try the opposite? Instead of building yourself up to a big ask, start with an unreasonable ask. It's important to make sure, however, that you don't actually want this unreasonable ask. You're expecting the other person to say no to this so that when you finally get to your smaller request, it seems a lot more reasonable. For example, let's say you're asking someone to donate to your charity. Start off by saying, "Would you be interested in making a $200 donation?" When they shake their head and say no, you can finally say, "We understand. In that case, how about just a $10 donation?"

### 4. Emphasize the benefits

To effectively convince someone of a course of action, you must consider the benefits they'll experience. Never assume that people will do anything simply out of the kindness of their hearts, especially if you're not a close friend or relative. When you're trying to persuade someone, really emphasize the benefits they'll receive if they agree to what you're saying. This works across the board, for all situations. If there's a reason they're reluctant, show them how one of the benefits will help them solve that problem. If you're trying to convince a coworker to get lunch with you, but he's too busy making last minute touches on a project, don't just emphasize how great the food will be. Be specific to his benefits. For example, you could say that he'll probably work much more efficiently once he eats some good food.

### 5. Speed up or slow down your speech

A known persuasion rule is that if an audience is most likely to disagree with what you're saying, increase the rate at which you're speaking. We see this a lot in salesmen where they will talk faster so that the person they're speaking to becomes overwhelmed with information. This gives them less time to notice things that may be incorrect and they are less likely to form a counter-argument.

If you think the odds are in your favor, the opposite will be beneficial. Slow down your speech if you think there's a strong possibility that your audience will agree with you. This will ensure that others feel more satisfied about their decision. If you give them time to assess all the information you've presented, they will feel as though they came to the conclusion completely on their own. They won't feel as though they were subjected to persuasion tactics, and this will make them happier with their decision.

## Three Tricks to Seduce Someone through Conversation

First of all, let's get one thing straight. If someone has zero attraction towards you, this section can't turn those tables. In fact, you'll be hard pressed to find anything that can. It can, however, turn a little bit of attraction into a lot of attraction. If there's something there, it can be kicked up a notch with these tips.

### 1. Fractionation

Fractionation is a Neuro-Linguistic Programming tool and its original intentions were not for seduction. In fact, it was used to enhance a patient's state of hypnosis during hypnotherapy. Today, it is thought to be a controversial technique for seduction, but one thing is for sure: it works. It involves using a hot-then-cold dynamic where desire is elevated through intermittent reinforcement.

It is easy to use this seduction method in an unethical way, but we don't advise resorting to abusive behavior. Instead, consider the many ethical ways we can use fractionation to stir desire.

- Incorporate hot-then-cold conversation topics. During ordinary conversation, we tend to start with light-hearted conversation. And if we care to prolong the interaction, it often deepens until it is at its most intense state, and both parties experience some level of exhaustion. When we use fractionation, we go back and forth between topics of intensity and topics that are more casual. It's up to you which one you start with, but you should always make the transition natural. Go from casual jokes, to discussion about your families, to lighthearted banter about TV shows, to heartbreak, and so on.

Make sure the serious topics bring your feelings into play, and the lighthearted topics should be factual or humorous. This rollercoaster of moods will intensify the feeling of intimacy. The other person will feel like they've shared everything with you, and you will earn their trust.

- Make push and pull statements. When making statements that both push and pull a partner, it's important to keep both sides equal. Too much of a push, and they'll think you're a mean person or simply not interested. Too much of a pull, and they'll think you're needy and clingy. Push and pull statements allow you to express your feelings without overwhelming someone. When done right, they can pique interest and enhance desire.

To formulate the ideal statement for your situation, choose an aspect of their personality to compliment (don't make up a good quality - really choose one she embodies) and turn a conventional response on its head. For example, you could say, "I hate how amazing you are at guitar. It's such a blow to my ego." It's also important to deliver this line with humor and playfulness, so they perceive it as positive instead of negative. Another example of such a statement is, "You dress so well, I'm starting to think you shouldn't be seen with me." Whatever you choose to say, make sure it does not come across as an insult.

## 2. Insinuation

Quite simply, insinuation is the act of planting a thought or idea in someone's head. Instead of forcing a direction, you simply let this carefully-planted seed grow on its own. When we use insinuation to seduce, we allow the object of our desire a quick glimpse of what we have in mind.

- Touch a person briefly, especially when they aren't expecting it. We advise doing this on a part of the body that is bound to send a tingle up their spine, though one should stay far away from all private regions. Lay a hand on the lower area of the back, affectionately rub someone's shoulder or grasp gently just above the knee.
- Make the occasional seductive glance, especially while keeping conversation light-hearted. Use your eyes to communicate how you truly feel, while your words stay in the safe zone.
- Use smart double entendres. The keyword here is 'smart.' Most people do not respond well to vulgar sexual innuendos, but a well-placed double entendre, at just the right time, can make a potential lover stir. It does not have to be sexual, it can be simply romantic. A double entendre is any statement that could have two meanings. If you're talking about your career, you could slip in the line, "I'm the kind of man who goes after what he wants and doesn't let go." This counts as a double entendre, since you could be talking about romantic pursuits as well. If you accompany this with an eye-gaze, you may just make the other person swoon. A sexual double entendre is a little riskier, but if you read the signals right, this could turn up the heat on your date.

### 3. Pauses

You know all about sexual tension, don't you? When we can't have someone exactly when we want them (and the feeling is mutual), our sense of desire grows and grows, until it's off-the-charts. As we've demonstrated, suspense enhances all emotion. And this is exactly why a well-timed and well-placed pause can be highly powerful. Here are some examples of when a pause can be effective.

- In a great compliment. Before you conclude the compliment, insert a pause that can be accompanied by eye-gazing or a shy smile. Let's say you're complimenting your current crush. You could say, "You look... stunning." This pause makes the compliment seem a lot more thoughtful and genuine, like you really thought about it, instead of just blurting it out.

- In a vulnerable statement. If you're discussing or explaining something in the realm of feelings, add a pause before the most revealing part of your sentence. This will add to the intimacy and vulnerability of the situation. If you're on a promising date, you could say, "I feel... like this is really going well." Pause. "Do you feel the same way?"

## Six Highly Effective Tips for Successful Negotiations

Negotiations most commonly happen with our employers or managers, but they are not restricted to the professional realm. When we're young, we may negotiate with our parents, and once we're older, we may negotiate with our partners. The sign of a successful negotiation is both parties walking away satisfied. Someone's goal is reached and the other side does not feel lesser for it. The other party may even feel it's for the best. To ensure your future negotiations are providing you and the people in your life with maximum benefits, keep these tips in mind.

1. **Make timing your ally**

Pay close attention to the frame of mind your negotiation will be met with. Timing can make all the difference between a successful deal and one that misses the mark. If you try to negotiate with someone who is rushing to another appointment, just heard bad news, or just finished a heated argument with another person, you are very likely not going to get the response you want.

**2. Do not use submissive or weak language**

When you find yourself in this situation with a superior, it may be tempting to use submissive language to soften your request. Before you begin negotiating, you may want to say "I hate to ask you this but..." or "I hope this isn't too much but..." so you don't come across as demanding. This can actually weaken your request. If the opposing negotiator has a streak of arrogance, they may even use your disclaimer against you and act more aggressive. Do not give them fodder to do that with. Be confident and assertive, knowing your full value. Avoid acting submissive but also steer clear of acting entitled. Find a balance between the two.

**3. Share honest information**

When you're in this situation, especially in a professional setting, it can be easy to feel like you should be guarded. This isn't true. Being honest with your employer or other authority figure can actually help your case. For example, if you need a raise because you feel you're not getting what you're worth, and perhaps you've started to struggle financially, this can give your boss more incentive to give you what you want.

**4. Always have a first offer in mind**

You're in a vulnerable position, so it's only natural to cringe at making the first offer. You may also think that it's wise to feel out the situation before any numbers are cast. Studies have shown, however, that those who make the first offer get closer to their goal. If you're looking for a raise, you're more likely to get your target salary if you have an offer in mind. This is because the first offer is what the negotiations revolve around. Instead of bending yourself to your employer's offer, they will bend themselves to yours. The first offer anchors the situation, so make sure it's yours.

### 5. Be brave with your offer

Make sure that your offer is not too low. People are often afraid to ask for too much, but studies have actually shown that you're more likely to low-ball yourself. Reflect on what your ideal outcome is and do not feel obligated to play it safe. Your ideal outcome may be more possible than you think!

### 6. Consider what they would gain from saying 'yes'

You can't walk into a room and just make demands. Unless the other party has something to gain from meeting your demands, you can kiss their cooperation goodbye. Before negotiating, consider the extent of their gain to figure out just how much you'll be able to ask for. This gain could be anything, from receiving better performance or improved efforts from you. Or perhaps the benefit is keeping you instead of losing you.

Don't shy away from using conversation to get what you want. The reality is: everyone is doing it. And guess what? You probably are too – just subconsciously. When we act subconsciously, our actions are not under our control, and anything could happen. Take control now and start getting the outcomes you desire.

# Conclusion

Congratulations on making it to the end of *Conversation Skills 2.0*! You should be proud of yourself and your newfound abilities. Social interactions can seem complex and overwhelming, but the new knowledge you've gleaned has placed you leagues ahead of the rest.

It's not that complicated once you break it down, is it? You'd do well to remember the big three rewards that we all look for in our human connections: safety, significance, and expansion. For the best outcomes, make your new acquaintances feel like they can trust you, like you appreciate them, and as though you have the ability to expand their horizons in some way, even if it's through humor and entertainment. Everything is grounded in these three major needs. Try and always satisfy them.

You've learned how to display likable behavior and give yourself an advantage for all proceeding conversations. In no time, you'll be brightening up a room and attracting connections like never before. You've also gained the tools for igniting interesting interactions, building magnetism, and developing deeper relationships with new and existing connections. And in addition to all of this, you've armored up for difficult social scenarios and learned persuasion techniques for a variety of social arenas.

Remember that it all begins with you. Learn to love yourself, stay true to who you are, and embrace your unique qualities. When we're comfortable with who we are, we let others in and we have more to offer them in our everyday conversations. Do what needs to be done to replenish your self-esteem and you'll easily stay a top-dog in your social interactions.

Another teaching I want you to take away is this: human beings are not as difficult as you think they are. Don't approach them with hesitation or fear. They are more similar to you than you realize, they've just accumulated different layers.

We can all be likened to locked treasure chests, filled with all manner of curious and fascinating things. Approach other humans the way you'd approach a locked treasure chest; take the time to find the right key and don't feel discouraged if one doesn't work. With patience, kindness, openness, and respect, try to experiment with different ways to open this box. What you find inside could be a great reward.

Human beings are social animals, so when we master conversation skills, connections are amplified and self-satisfaction becomes the new norm. Isn't that a reality you'd like to see?

# RELATIONSHIP COMMUNICATION

Mistakes Every Couple Makes & How to Fix Them. Discover How to Resolve Any Conflict with Your Partner & Create Deeper Intimacy in Your Relationship

# Table of Contents

**Introduction** .................................................................................. **131**

**Chapter One - Relationships 101** ............................................. **134**
    The Vital Needs Every Relationship Must Fulfill ........................ 135
    The Five Stages of a Relationship .................................................. 140

**Chapter Two - The Diagnosis** ................................................... **145**
    6 Big Signs You and Your Partner Need to Communicate Better ... 145
    The Reasons Why We Don't Communicate ..................................... 147
    The 10 Communication Mistakes You Don't Know You're Making
    ................................................................................................................. 149

**Chapter Three - Habits for Happiness** ................................... **154**
    9 Communication Habits that Save Relationships .......................... 154
    All About the 80/20 Rule ................................................................. 159
    Measuring Your Happiness with the Magic Relationship Ratio ...... 159
    Stop Freaking Out About these 6 "Problems" ................................. 160

**Chapter Four - Love in Every Way** ......................................... **165**
    All You Need to Know about Love Languages ............................... 165
    How to Use Nonverbal Communication to your Advantage ........... 168
    Less-Known but Powerful Ways to Show Your Partner Love ........ 170

**Chapter Five - Decoding Your Partner** ................................... **175**
    Understanding Your Partner's Particular Needs ............................. 176
    5 Absolutely Essential Things to Do When Your Partner Has
    Experienced Trauma ........................................................................ 179

**Chapter Six - It's All About You** .............................................. **183**
    How to Instantly Become a Better Partner ..................................... 183
    Understanding Your Relationship Attachment Style ...................... 188

Relationship Communication

Must-Know Tips for Starting a New Relationship When You Have a History of Bad Relationships .................................................................. 191

**Chapter Seven - The Ticking Time Bomb**.................................... **196**

When to Press the Pause or Stop Button .........................................196

How to Bring Up Your Concerns the Right Way...............................200

5 Statements to Instantly Defuse a Heated Discussion.....................202

What NOT to Say During an Argument...........................................204

9 Relationship Problems You Cannot Fix .......................................205

**Chapter Eight - Deepening the Bond**........................................... **211**

Exercises and Activities that Strengthen Relationships ....................211

Bond Instantly with these 8 Fun Couple Activities...........................217

**Conclusion** ................................................................................... **222**

# Introduction

Remember the first time you laid eyes on your significant other? It might not have been love at first sight, and maybe not even second sight, but I'm willing to bet on one thing: you thought winning them over would be the biggest challenge. You wanted so badly to get that date and when you finally succeeded in getting it, you wondered what you could do to get them to really like you. Now, months or years down the road, just when you thought it would all be smooth-sailing, you've found the puzzle only gets more confusing. Now, you realize winning them over was the easy part. Coexisting happily? That's a whole different ballpark.

Communication was simple when it was all sweet nothings and getting to know each other. Now that you're closer, there are different things on your mind. You have concerns, you have unmet needs, and you've noticed other ways you'd like to improve your relationship. Chances are that your significant other feels exactly the same way.

The problem is that these concerns are never easy things to express. If done incorrectly, it could hurt your partner's feelings and do irreparable damage. And yet if you don't express yourself, you just might explode, also doing irreparable damage. You're feeling a little cornered, aren't you? I don't blame you.

Your mind is probably swirling with a million questions like, "How can I communicate with my partner in the most effective way possible? How can I go about maintaining my happiness as well as his or her happiness? And how on earth can I do all this without completely exhausting myself?"

Even if you have pretty good communication already, why stop there? Aim for the stars. Your relationship deserves it.

# Relationship Communication

Studies have shown that poor communication is one of the major reasons why a relationship fails. Many of those relationships could have been saved if they had this guide in their lives. A relationship ended over bad communication is a relationship that could have been saved. We can all learn to communicate better, no matter how shy or ineffective we may be now. All we need are the right tools and motivation. The fact you're here now proves there's a high chance you already have the motivation. Good for you. Now all you need is the expert advice. That's where I come in.

I've spent key years of my life studying the way humans interact with each other – how to use each gesture or glance as a key to a person's true feelings and intentions. I've paid close attention to the way individuals communicate and I've unlocked the secrets to what succeeds, and what inevitably fails. By staying attuned to the needs of others, I've discovered little-known tricks that can instantly shift a tense dynamic to an open, loving one. I've gained my expertise by staying aware of what works and what doesn't. I've watched relationships deteriorate over poorly phrased sentences, and I've seen couples reignite their love with just a few words. I've tested my methods on couples on the brink, and I've watched them blossom into their best selves. Even today, couples I've worked with continue to thank me. You see, once you have the tools, you're set for life.

With my help, you and your partner are one-step closer to the fantasy you both share – the one where you can say anything to each other and solve absolutely any problem together. You may not know you share this fantasy, but you do. When communication is strained, both partners desperately wish it could be better. You may think they don't notice, but trust me, they notice as much as you do. With my help, you'll make great communication the new norm. You'll start a brand new chapter where you can look back and think, "I can't believe how far we've come!" This book will strengthen you and your partner as a team. And do you want to know something else? A great team can do absolutely anything together.

Don't let this opportunity for growth pass you by. I've known many couples to express deep regret when they know they didn't try as hard as they could have. They continue to be haunted by times they were offered good advice and they said, "Maybe later." Truth is, the longer you wait to make these changes, the more stuck you become in your old ways. The longer you communicate to your partner in the wrong way (or don't communicate at all), the more hurt and strain your relationship accumulates. How much longer before your love breaks under the weight of it?

Choose love and choose your partner, by saying 'yes' to better relationship communication skills. Your new, happier future together is so close – it starts on the next page! So what are you waiting for?

# Chapter One - Relationships 101

If there's one topic that dominates music, literature, film, you name it, it's without a doubt our romantic relationships. Do you ever wonder why this is? Romantic love is certainly not the strongest emotion we feel, and new parents would argue it's not even the strongest form of love. So why then do we continue to write and make art about it? The answer is simple: it's because we still don't understand it.

Romance and relationships are some of the most puzzling aspects of our lives. Feelings of attraction can come on unexpectedly, causing confusion and taking over our rational minds. Sometimes we have these feelings when it makes no sense at all to feel them. Swept up in new, burning romances, people can behave unlike their true selves and lose sight of their better judgment. And when we get into relationships, we enter a whole new realm of emotional confusion.

There's a bit of a paradox, isn't there? We get to know our significant others very well, and at the same time, we become more aware of how much we don't know. They are the people we know best of all, and yet they can also be the biggest mysteries. We may know their emotional responses, their habits, their tics, but rarely do we know *why* they are this way. Better communication is how we eliminate this distance.

Before we dive in, let's take a quick pause and remember something profoundly important: two halves make a whole. For a relationship to succeed, two individuals need to hold up their side of the equation. This doesn't just mean taking turns washing the dishes or splitting the bill. It means doing the self-work to be a better partner. It means reflecting on your needs and wants, your behavior, and considering how to be better when you're confronted with your dysfunctions.

So let's go to step one. Remember when we mentioned reflecting on our needs? Before we can begin to communicate our needs and wants, we must first know what our basic needs are.

## The Vital Needs Every Relationship Must Fulfill

As complicated as relationships may seem, our basic needs are fairly easy to categorize. For a relationship to thrive, there are five basic but very important needs that should be met for both partners. Please note these basic needs aren't the only needs we have, they are just the ones we all share. Each individual has unique needs, depending on their personality and background, but for simplicity's sake, we'll start with the basics.

You may encounter certain personalities that have a higher tolerance for the lack of one of these needs. For example, have you ever met a boring couple that seemed just fine, despite their lack of variety? Or a couple that stimulated each other intellectually, but didn't have a true emotional connection? Many couples can make it work without taking care of all five needs. But the big questions remain: are they truly happy? Couldn't they be happier?

**The Need to Feel and Be Secure**

Without this need, a relationship is nothing. It's the most basic of the five and it refers to our deep need to feel emotionally, physically, and psychologically intact. If your significant other claims this need is not being met, serious work needs to be done. Feeling a lack of security could indicate a few types of problems: our physical well-being is threatened or we are being emotionally abused on some level. It all comes down to one partner feeling hurt and anticipating being hurt again, sometimes going through huge lengths to avoid it.

Many people don't realize this need is unmet because they think abuse is always intentional. This isn't true at all. Many partners don't realize they're using emotionally abusive tactics such as gaslighting or manipulation. They may have these responses wired into their brain without realizing how much damage it does.

***When your need to feel secure isn't being met...***

You feel like you can't be vulnerable around your partner. You fear they may verbally or physically hurt you if things don't go their way. You worry that instead of being met with love, you'll encounter more pain or distress. You constantly think of how they are going to react in response to something you do or say; this prevents you from expressing what you need to express. You fear that if you're honest about how you feel, you will be dismissed, mocked, or you might incite anger. You get the distinct feeling that if you share your needs, you will receive a negative response.

**The Need to Feel Significant**

Let's clear up a misconception: security and significance are not the same things. You may have total confidence that your partner won't hurt you, but is this enough to feel valued and special? It shouldn't be. Giving someone security is common decency, but showing them they're significant is a loving act. When our partner makes us feel significant and special, we feel good about ourselves and are overcome with warmth, knowing everything we give them is appreciated. We feel like the love we give is being received, and not just draining through a bottomless pit. This, in turn, encourages us to show even more love.

A person who has been cheated on is an example of someone who has had their need for significance compromised. There's no worse way to show someone they aren't special than by getting involved with another person behind their back.

When we get into a fight, we can continue to show our partners they're special by apologizing when we do something wrong. This shows we considered their feelings, tried to see their point of view, and are trying to make up for our wrongdoing. Show your partner love and appreciation. Otherwise, what's the point?

Make your partner feel significant by showing them love, and responding to their loving gestures with appreciation and affection.

***When your need to feel significant isn't being met...***

You find yourself worrying about your partner's infidelity or whether they truly love you. You may start to feel disposable, like your partner doesn't really see you for who you are. You don't feel particularly special in your partner's life. You feel like you serve a function, and not much more than that. You find yourself overcome by the feeling that you've given them everything, yet it's still somehow not enough.

**The Need for Variety**

When we get to know someone extremely well, our lives begin to form a routine. This is a normal occurrence, and unfortunately, the boredom that arises from it is normal too. To keep a relationship healthy and both partners happy, it's vital that we switch things up every once in a while. Studies have shown that we feel closer to our partners when engage in stimulating activities together.

This could mean anything: going out for dinner instead of cooking, signing up for a fun activity instead of staying home, or even doing something new in the bedroom. Whatever is part of your normal routine, do something completely different.

When both partners have busy work or family lives, a routine is inevitable. But it's completely within your power to make sure it doesn't become boring. Reignite the fire by adding a little more adventure!

***When your need for variety isn't being met…***

You don't feel as excited by your partner as you used to. It feels like you're stuck in a loop. It feels like your life together is just a series of tasks that need to get finished. It's been a while since you experienced a rush or a thrill together. A part of you longs to feel what you felt at the beginning of your relationship.

**The Need for Emotional Connection**

If a relationship is going to make it long-term, emotional intimacy is profoundly important. To maintain any close relationship in our lives, we need to make time to connect and allow ourselves to relate to each other. Sometimes this can come very easily to two people, but it's also completely normal for some couples to have to try a little harder. This doesn't mean you're any less meant for each other. Cultural, background, or personality differences can all be contributing factors to two people being more reticent. Start by sharing something honest and vulnerable, and invite your partner to share something similar.

***When your need for emotional connection isn't being met…***

Your partner sometimes seems like a mystery and there are times it feels like you don't really know them. You get the distinct feeling they don't understand you, and you, too, find their actions puzzling and confusing. You spend a lot of time wondering about them and why they do what they do. You may also feel there's something they need to say, but they're resisting saying it. You also feel the urge to share and open up, but there's never quite enough time. It all gets swept up in another moment.

## Relationship Communication

**The Need for Personal Expansion**

If your relationship ticks the above four boxes, good for you. You've got a good relationship in your life. Want to know how to make it better? Give each other opportunities for expansion. In other words, help each other grow. Personal expansion can come in many forms, but essentially, we satisfy this need by feeling we've learned something or are learning something from one another.

In a healthy relationship, both partners encourage each other to be the best versions of themselves. They do not act complacent about their partner's goals or achievements, and they certainly do not put each other down. Give your partner positive, gentle feedback and constructive criticism.

Another way we fulfill this need is by stimulating our partner intellectually. Get into a discussion and teach each other new things. Expand each others' minds. Believe it or not, this all comes down to our biological need to procreate for further evolution. We want to find a partner we can truly collaborate with; someone who brings evolved qualities to the table or will evolve with us.

*When your need for personal expansion isn't being met...*

Your partner makes you feel stagnant. Sometimes you even wonder if they're holding you back from what you could truly accomplish. They don't inspire you in any way. When you get into discussions, it doesn't always feel like you're on the same page. You're often bored or confused by what they talk about. You don't think your partner is very wise or very smart.

## The Five Stages of a Relationship

After studying hundreds of different couples, well-known relationship coach, Dr. Susan Campbell, noticed something interesting: just like human beings, relationships have their own lifetimes, made of five different stages. Each stage has its own distinct patterns and with a little self-awareness, all couples will be able to identify where exactly their relationship is.

Unlike with human beings, however, each stage will vary in length from couple to couple. And not every couple is lucky enough to learn the lessons of every single stage, especially the hardest stage of them all, Stage Two. To ensure you and your significant other power through these levels with love, trust, and grace, it's best to inform yourself on what they are.

**STAGE ONE: Romance & Attraction**

Of all the stages, this is the one you likely know most about. Hollywood films have convinced many people that stage one is what relationships are like all the time – but this could not be further from the truth. At this early point in the relationship, both partners are completely infatuated by each other. We still see each other through rose-tinted glasses, only seeing the positive aspects of our partner while in denial about their negative traits. Here, we still don't quite see our partners exactly as they are.

Your five needs are suspended in this stage because we are less likely to notice if they're not being fulfilled. We're more likely to shrug things off and give our partners the benefit of the doubt because the relationship is so new. We are very easily satisfied at this stage, choosing to see what we want to see.

The length of this stage varies wildly. Some couples progress to the next level after as little as two months and for some lucky couples, it can last up to two years – but rarely longer than that. Stage one generally lasts until partners decide to declare some sort of permanence. For some people, this is when they decide to start dating exclusively, and for others, it may be moving in together. How permanence is perceived varies from person to person.

**STAGE TWO: Disillusionment & Struggle**

After the euphoria and rush of stage one, we progress to the most difficult part of our relationship. This is when the rose-tinted glasses come off for the first time. We finally begin to see our partner and relationship as they are, and disappointment will begin to seep in. One or both partners will begin to long for how things were at the beginning of the relationship. This is where the balancing act comes in: how can we maintain our personal freedom while also being a good partner?

It's important to remember that going through this is completely normal. Because the media has given us such an unrealistic idea of love, we tend to jump to conclusions at the second stage. As soon as we encounter these problems, we think the relationship must be doomed. I'll tell you now: most problems that occur at this stage *can* be fixed!

To progress to the next stage, it's crucial that partners learn to:

- Accept each other for who they are and not who they want them to be.
- Come to an agreement and compromise about the behaviors and habits creating tension in the relationship.
- Acquire tools and strategies for positive self-transformation.
- Communicate honestly, kindly, and constructively.
- Embrace change and stop trying to fight it.

All at once, our needs come into play. If a need isn't being met, this is where we begin to feel that something is wrong. And if we're at all self-aware, we'll know exactly what this need is. Solving unmet needs now is the key to meeting them long-term.

Most divorces and break-ups happen during this period. It can last months or sometimes even years. Couples can be together for a long time and remain stuck in this stage, unhappy until they finally decide to part. Individuals are tested at this stage. How we choose to act and treat each other will determine the course our relationship takes. If we reject the lessons we need to learn, these problems may surface again in the next relationship.

**STAGE THREE: Stability & Mutual Respect**

If you make it through the storm, congratulations. There's more peace and harmony in stage three. Here, relationships have matured in a big way and both partners, whether they realize it or not, are better versions of themselves. Strategies are used and compromises are respected. Instead of trying desperately to change your partner, you focus on what's in your control. Let's use an example:

At stage two, Sam and Diane were constantly fighting. Diane would come home from work and see him sprawled in front of the sofa, watching violent TV shows and with an array of junk food spread out on the coffee table. This was his after-work routine. Sam wanted to relax and feel at home, but Diane wanted things to be cleaner and more organized. In their fights, Sam called Diane too strict and controlling, and she called him a messy slob.

At stage three, Sam and Diane have accepted each other's different needs. Diane now understands that Sam needs to let loose in order to de-stress from work. Sam also understands that Diane needs to see a clean and quiet environment to de-stress from her own job. The solution? On some nights, Sam can unwind how he wants, but he puts the TV volume lower so Diane can use a meditation app in the next room. Other nights, Diane can read in peace and quiet, while Sam watches his TV shows using headphones in the next room. And on special nights, they'll watch a show they both want to see and get snacks they both enjoy. If anything bothers them, they'll bring it up gently and kindly, without putting the other person down.

In stage three, you've decided to compromise and you are now adjusting to life with these new changes implemented. You are finally beginning to understand what makes a good partner. You no longer see compromises as infringements on your personal freedom, instead, you see them as opportunities for cooperation. All conflicts that arise are dealt with maturely.

The needs for emotional connection and personal growth are likely well-met during this stage. To avoid becoming bored and stagnant, make sure there's a healthy dose of variety.

## STAGE FOUR: Love & Commitment

Here, love is fully-formed. All our actions spell out our commitment to our significant other. Not only have you accepted each other and learned to compromise, you've accepted your life together as *your life*. This doesn't always mean marriage, but it is here that two partners are truly ready for marriage. In stage three, we accept our partner's idiosyncrasies, but in stage four, we love and embrace these differences.

Couples will still experience tension and conflict in this stage, but this is usually circumstantial or incited by new life events. Here, they've already worked out a dynamic for the situations they know well, but inevitably, situations they're not prepared for arise.

For example, Sam and Diane no longer get into heated arguments about how to behave at home. However, one evening at a dinner party, Sam told a story about Diane that really embarrassed her. He thought it would be funny but she argued it was too personal. Conflict like this is bound to arise sometimes, but using the tools they've learned in Stage Two, they can come to a resolution.

At this stage, it's important that partners make sure their needs for variety and emotional connection are met. The commitment has been solidified and sometimes this can mean the routine has begun to control their life.

**STAGE FIVE: Symbiosis & Sharing**

When we reach the final stage of our relationship, we are no longer insular and contained. Here, we begin to work together to give back something to the world. Once a strong foundation has been built, it's natural to want to build upwards and outwards.

This can mean children, but not for every couple. It can also mean starting a project or business. You know a couple is in this stage when they have a giving, almost parental quality to them or they just seem to *get things done* together. It's the opposite of two young lovebirds locking themselves in a room and not talking to anyone; a solid couple wants to share with the world in some form. They are ready to collaborate in every way.

# Chapter Two - The Diagnosis

Think of the last time you went to the doctor. It doesn't matter what it was for, whether it was serious or completely mild, every single time you've had to be surveyed for a diagnosis. Before any solutions can be arrived at or any treatment administered, the symptoms must be noted and analyzed. It doesn't matter how potent the medicine is; if it's treating an ailment you don't have, it won't fix what's really wrong with you.

This same principle applies here. You can read up on great relationship advice, but not all of it will be helpful for your specific situation. If you want to improve your relationship, you're going to need to get real about what the issues are. The following chapter will focus on identifying your relationship's problem points. Be honest with yourself. The signs are there, you just need to notice them.

## 6 Big Signs You and Your Partner Need to Communicate Better

### 1. You talk about your partner more than you talk to them

It's completely normal to discuss our relationship with our friends and family, especially when we need advice, but consider this important question: do you ever share these same issues directly with your partner? How much do your communications *about* your partner outweigh your communications *with* them?

### 2. You've become irritable around your partner or vice versa

At one point in your relationship, it seemed like your partner could do anything and you'd let it blow past you. But now, it takes a lot less for you to lose your patience with them. You find yourself becoming irritated over small things that never used to bother you before. This is a key sign one of your needs is not being met, and a warning sign that you need to open up about it before you snap. Be honest with yourself and consider the real reason behind your lowered tolerance.

### 3. You find yourself wondering what your partner is truly feeling

We should never feel like our partner is a total mystery. If you frequently find yourself trying to figure out your partner like they're a complicated puzzle, then there's a lot that needs to be cleared up between you two. In a healthy relationship with great communication, we're on the same page as our partners 99% of the time.

### 4. You and/or your partner are prone to stonewalling

When one partner shuts down, refuses to be vulnerable and cooperate, this is called stonewalling. This goes deeper than the silent treatment. Someone who is stonewalling you will still speak to you, but you'll get the distinct feeling they have their guard up. They're not being real and they may even be playing games. A person who stonewalls is not communicating something that needs to be shared. Why else would they have such a strong reaction to being vulnerable?

### 5. You avoid certain topics and feel like you're walking on eggshells

Sometimes there is more than one elephant in the room. Sometimes it may even feel more like a mammoth. Does the room feel heavy with words unsaid? Is there noticeable tension? This is a big sign that the relationship is struggling with open communication. For some reason, neither partner is comfortable just saying what needs to be said. And chances are, this isn't the only thing they're struggling to say.

### 6. One or both partners is being passive-aggressive

Passive-aggression is a big sign that something needs to be said. It occurs when someone does not want to be obnoxious or outright aggressive, so they try to air their grievances without being completely upfront. They're not really being honest, they are trying to talk about it without *really* talking about it. Sarcasm is another form of passive-aggression when it is used in a nasty way. Whenever we can't communicate directly, we find more indirect ways of making our feelings known.

## The Reasons Why We Don't Communicate

Knowing the reason behind poor communication won't give us the tools we need, but it'll show us where to begin working. How can we expect to get anywhere if we don't know where to start?

- **One or both partners has trouble being vulnerable**

This is a common reason why people don't communicate and it is an obstacle that can be overcome with practice. There are many extremely valid reasons why someone may have trouble being vulnerable. Sometimes there's a history of abuse, cultural differences, an oppressive upbringing, or maybe it's just that person's personality.

- **You're scared of being criticized**

When we're in a relationship with a highly critical person, this can affect our ability to be open with them. We're less likely to be honest because we'll constantly be thinking about how they'll react to our honest thoughts. Even if it's something that won't upset them at all, we may over-anticipate this reaction out of anxiety. It's important that the critical partner is identified in this scenario.

- **You don't realize there's something you need to say**

Many people in the world have been taught to live with a 'get up and move on' sort of attitude. While this is a great way to approach life's problems, it can cause communication to suffer in a relationship. Why? Because this attitude gets us in the habit of just swallowing our pain and distress, without acknowledging it. We try to suppress these feelings and in doing so, we become less self-aware about how we truly feel. So when there's something we desperately need to bring up with our partner, we may not be aware of what it really is. This can result in a lot of backhanded and passive-aggressive behavior.

- **Your lives have become busy**

When we're busy, we don't just fail to communicate because we literally have less time to talk. Having less time with our partner means we also start to lose a sense of intimacy. They're not around so we are no longer able to feed our connection. When we feel distant from our partners, we are less likely to want to share something personal with them.

- **One of you is keeping a secret**

It's a possibility we don't like to consider, but it remains a potentiality for any couple. When we have something to hide, it can take a toll on communication as a whole. Subconsciously or fully consciously, the partner with the secret starts to keep their distance, knowing that it's the only way they can protect their secret. Often, their significant other will also sense that something is off, which only leads to greater distance and even worse communication. This secret is not always a betrayal like infidelity.

- **You're holding onto resentment**

When one partner is holding onto a grudge, they stop allowing themselves to connect with their significant other. The grudge could be over something silly or something huge, but it always has the same effect. Resentment is so strong it can almost feel like a third entity in the relationship. Even if we verbalize that we've forgiven our partner, as long as there's any ounce of resentment, this forgiveness is not entirely present. When we secretly or not-so-secretly hold a grudge, communication can feel strained or completely nonexistent. The partner on the receiving end will feel like there's a wall they can't get past.

# The 10 Communication Mistakes You Don't Know You're Making

Another beginner's step to improving relationship communication is to look at what's impeding progress. Before we can even think about remedies and solutions, we need to identify what behavior absolutely needs to go. It's time to be honest with yourself.

1. **You're refusing to be accountable for anything**

When we're faced with a situation that distresses us, it's difficult to accept we played a part in making it happen. But the harsh reality is we usually do. When we're in a relationship, it is vital that we learn to take accountability for our part in a situation. Apologies don't mean anything if there isn't accountability to back it up. When we learn to own up to our actions, we create a safe space of honesty, vulnerability, and kindness in our relationship. It reinforces the idea that you're a team. Yes, you both played a part in creating an unfavorable circumstance, but most importantly, you can both work together to prevent it in the future. Don't treat your partner like the villain; treat them like your team member.

## 2. You're dismissing your partner's feelings

Here's a secret you likely already know: sometimes you're going to think your partner's feelings are ridiculous. Sometimes, you won't understand them at all and you may have the urge to just walk away. It's important to stress, however, that you should *never* walk away or shrug them off. Dismissing your partner's feelings can do a lot of damage. You need to understand that even if it doesn't mean anything to you, it could be causing your partner a lot of pain. When you dismiss your partner's feelings you're telling them you don't care about how they feel. This can create even deeper pain for them and ruin communication in your relationship.

## 3. You're using harsh or abusive language

You could be saying something completely reasonable, but if you're using abusive language or calling them names to make your point, you're doing yourself and your partner a disservice. When we use abusive language to convey a message, it is far less likely to be heard. No one wants to be scolded like a child or made to feel like a failure. The language and tone we use should encourage our partner to do better, not shame them for what they've done. As soon as we do this, we make it more likely for our partners to act out of fear, instead of empowerment and love. This type of behavior can ruin a relationship and in some cases, it can even traumatize the person on the receiving end. It is essential to fix this behavior as soon as it arises.

## 4. You're yelling and screaming

If you're raising your voice or yelling at your partner, you're killing all chances of seeing eye-to-eye. Just like using abusive language, this is the wrong way to deliver a message. It doesn't matter how

## Relationship Communication

rational that message is or how right you are; when you yell and scream, you make your message less powerful. The delivery of your message should encourage your partner to cooperate with you, not cower in fear. When we act with aggression, we increase the likelihood of our partner's reacting with defensiveness. As soon as we do this, we enter combat mode. Nothing gets solved when we are in combat mode.

### 5. You always concede and apologize

It's not always about being too aggressive, you can also be too submissive. If you find yourself constantly agreeing and apologizing even though you didn't do anything wrong, you're taking the easy way out. It's true that we should pick our battles and sometimes it's more important to swallow our ego instead of arguing, but this shouldn't be a common occurrence. If you find yourself constantly running into the same problem with your partner, it's time to stop backing down so easily. If you continue to take the blame, the problem will never get solved because you're not the person who's causing it. For the sake of the relationship, you need to tell your partner how they are creating the situation at hand. Help them see the opportunity to make things better.

### 6. You throw around absolutes

Throwing around words like 'always' or 'never' when you don't mean it literally can sometimes be detrimental to the situation at hand. For example, if you say to your partner, "You're always whining" or "You never help me with anything" this is likely not an accurate statement. If it's not literally true, it can come across as hurtful because you're exaggerating the problem. It's essential that you stick to the facts when you're bringing up a problem, and steer-clear of finger-pointing language.

### 7. You're being *too* honest

We always hear that we should never keep anything from our partner, but that's not entirely true. It is possible to be *too* honest and it can cause a great deal of damage. As a rule of thumb, it's usually a good idea to be honest about something that you *did,* but it's not always necessary to tell them everything you *think.* If you're planning on having lunch with an ex, you should absolutely be honest about this. But should you tell your partner you find one of their friends attractive? Definitely not. This type of honesty can hurt someone's feelings.

### 8. You're not allowing yourself to be vulnerable

It's normal to feel some resistance towards being vulnerable. After all, we're giving someone very personal information and it's natural to want to protect ourselves. But for a relationship to be healthy, it's vital that we learn to be vulnerable with our partner. All this means is we need to share how we feel in an honest and open manner. It means showing a side of ourselves that we don't normally show anyone. To truly achieve a sense of intimacy, we need to let people in. Avoid communicating enigmatically or using sarcasm and humor in serious situations.

### 9. You're expecting your partner to read your mind

This is a common reason why people get mad at each other and it's easily prevented. The frustration stems from the idea that our partners should just *know* when something is wrong, and they should just *know* what to do to fix it. This is not at all fair to your significant other. Of course your emotions and needs seem obvious to you. After all, you're the one feeling them! There are many reasons your partner wouldn't notice and most of them are not worth getting mad over. The fact of the matter is when you're not expecting someone to have a certain reaction, you're less likely to notice the signs. So give your

## Relationship Communication

partner a break and just be honest. Once you get the problem out of the way, you can start working on solutions.

**10. You attack your partner and not the issue**

When our significant others do something that bothers us, it can be tempting to start attacking their character, but we should never do this. Let's say they completely forgot to pick up groceries on the way home from work. As maddening as this can be, do not say, "You're so forgetful. You forget everything!" Even if they do have a tendency to forget, always focus on the issue at hand. Instead of calling them forgetful, bring up what's really inciting your anger in this specific situation, i.e. forgetting the groceries. Consider saying something like, "I really wish you'd try harder to remember these important errands. I would feel much better if we could share the task of picking up groceries." You could even offer a solution like creating a phone reminder. You could also take some accountability and add, "I should have texted you to remind you. I know you have a lot on your mind after work." When we attack our partner's character, this is a put-down. It can make them feel terrible about themselves and this isn't helpful in creating a solution.

How many of these problems and signs have you recognized in your relationship? The more that you resonate with, the more desperately your relationship needs better communication. And don't worry, most of this is completely fixable!

# Chapter Three - Habits for Happiness

The power of baby steps is highly underrated. Just think about it – our lives are not made of big achievements and end-destinations. It's made of the smaller struggles, the day-to-day grind, and the little victories that accumulate into big victories.

One of the major ways we set ourselves up for failure is by focusing on the end result and not the small steps that get us there. For example, we may say we want to lose weight, but instead of creating achievable step-by-step goals like "Only have dessert once a week" or "Eat one salad every day," we'll create big goals like "Lose 5 lbs in one week" without a single method to help our progress.

The secret to achieving anything is this: create good habits that support your goal. Want fantastic communication in your relationship? It's probably not going to be excellent immediately. And progress will be slow if you don't plan smaller, achievable steps. If you want better communication, you'll need to create better communication habits. It starts with implementing one technique, then another, and learning to make these new tools part of your routine. To succeed, you need to reinvent your norms.

## 9 Communication Habits that Save Relationships

### 1. Check-in with each other every day

This act is so simple, yet so powerful. At least once per day, get an update on how your partner is doing. This doesn't always mean asking "How are you?" it can also mean asking how their day was when you see each other after work. If you remember your partner mentioning a difficult upcoming meeting, ask how that meeting went. By doing this, we show our significant other we care and that we are listening.

## Relationship Communication

### 2. Learn to use "I feel/It feels" statements

When you start a statement with "I feel" it turns a potentially accusatory or assumptive statement into something more gentle. For the best possible outcome in any situation, especially when one partner is in a tender state, "I feel" statements are the best way to communicate with them. Notice the difference between these two statements:

- "You're not listening to me. You haven't heard anything I've said."
- "I feel like you're not listening to me. It feels like you haven't heard anything I've said."

Switch the emphasis from "you" to "I." Notice how this makes something that could be interpreted as accusatory or aggressive suddenly becomes an honest observation. You're not telling your partner how they acted; you are emphasizing how you are experiencing their actions. There's a big difference. This is harder to argue with because when we explain how we feel, we become vulnerable. Since we are just saying "it feels" that way, we give our partner the opportunity to say that's not what they meant. When we don't use "it feels," we corner our partner, making their cooperation less likely.

### 3. Reconsider what you deem 'unimportant'

This less-known tip is remarkably effective at transforming relationships. When our partner says something we don't think is that important, we fail to make one massive realization: it could be very important to them! Whenever you're about to say "That's nice, honey" or perhaps even ignoring what they say altogether, consider the positive impact a proper response would have. If your partner just got home from work and she mentions in passing that she made a new friend, do not just nod and say "Oh, cool." Say enthusiastically, "That's wonderful you made a new friend."

Want to know something else? If your partner shows enthusiasm, even if it's for something small, you must meet that enthusiasm with interest or at the very least, you must acknowledge it properly. If you're taking a walk and your partner says, "Oh look! What a pretty bird!" it's very likely that you don't really care about the pretty bird. But you should still never ignore your partner when they are excited about something. Say "I wonder what kind of bird that is" or just agree with them by saying, "That is a very pretty bird, indeed." You should respond at least once to their statement.

All of this creates a closer connection and allows your partner to feel truly significant. It diminishes feelings of being ignored and unnoticed. If your partner's need for significance is not being met, this is a habit you should implement into your daily communication.

### 4. Ask them questions about their interests

Get in the habit of asking your partner about topics or events that interest them. I don't just mean subjects that they sort-of think are interesting, but the topics that get them really excited, even if they're a little silly. If your partner is into celebrity gossip, ask them what their favorite celebrity is up to lately, or ask what they thought of the latest article about them.

Think of the last time you saw your partner's eyes light up when they were talking. That's a good place to start. When we get into the habit of doing this, we build a stronger connection with our partners. It makes them feel special because you not only remember what they love, but you care enough to let them talk about it. As they speak, show genuine enthusiasm for what they're saying.

### 5. Say at least one positive or encouraging thing to your partner every day

It doesn't have to be a long, drawn-out love letter; just say at least one positive thing to your partner daily, even if it's short and sweet.

It can be anything, and it should be spoken with enthusiasm. You're also free to do this by text. Some ideas are:

- "You've been working so hard lately. You know, I really admire what a hard-worker you are."
- "I know you've been stressed out, but I think you're handling everything very well."
- "You look wonderful today."

If you can't think of anything, then why not a simple but heartfelt "I love you"? Pepper more positive statements into your daily communication with your partner and you'll find your entire dynamic instantly becomes more loving.

### 6. If you disagree, gently invite them to reflect

You can't avoid disagreements with your partner, but you *can* avoid turning them into full-blown arguments. Instead of "you should" or "you shouldn't" statements, encourage them to reflect. Don't push an idea on them, lead them to it.

Let's use an example. Kelly has planned a lunch date with a friend that has always put her down and been mean to her. Her partner, James, doesn't think it's a good idea for them to meet up. Instead of saying, "You shouldn't meet up with her," he chooses to incite reflection. He asks, "Do you think she'll behave the same way she did last time?" and "What do you think will be different this time?" James allows his opinion to be known by using "I" statements. He says, "I just worry that she'll be a bad friend, like she normally is. I don't like to see you upset."

Use questions to invite your partner to reflect, and if you must add your opinion, always use "I" statements.

### 7. Still say 'please' and 'thank you'

When we stop using our basic manners with someone, it's a troubling sign that we've started to take them for granted. Make sure that no matter what happens you are always in the habit of saying 'please' and 'thank you' at the appropriate moments. Even if you're in a bad mood, you should still say it. This is the most basic way to show appreciation for someone, and when we stop, we display a sense of entitlement. You may think your partner won't notice but they will, especially when they've put considerable effort into providing you with something. Always show appreciation for your partner's efforts and adhere to these basic good manners.

## 8. Engage in pillow talk

Even when both partners have busy schedules, there's no reason they can't enjoy a little pillow talk. After all, we all need to go to bed at some point! Pillow talk occurs at the end of the day, when couples are winding down in bed. It consists of intimate and relaxed conversation where both partners can share their thoughts. Couples can choose to cuddle or not, but physical contact tends to create a more loving atmosphere. If you're having a somewhat tense conversation, cuddling can reduce combativeness and increase the likelihood of cooperation. When couples get in the habit of engaging in pillow talk, they have a greater chance at keeping the intimacy and connection alive in their relationship.

## 9. Share openly with your partner

To create a greater sense of intimacy and connection, don't wait to be asked questions – just start sharing interesting parts of your day. Tell them about funny things that happened at work, or about that hilarious text your friend sent you. If you're upset by something that happened, be vulnerable and share it with them. Once you start doing this you create an environment where sharing and openness is not just welcome, but completely normal. This means your partner is more likely to share with you as well. When distance grows between two people, they tend to overthink how to make it better. The solution is simple: just start acting like there's no distance at all.

When you share openly with your partner, make sure there's an opening for them to share as well. Do not spend hours talking about just you and your day. Invite them to share things that are exciting or interesting in their life. Of course, some of us are naturally more talkative, and at times, we just can't help it. To ensure that there's an even exchange of conversation, consider the following technique:

## All About the 80/20 Rule

If you normally do most of the talking or you sense your partner needs to get something off their chest, opt for the 80/20 rule. This technique is extremely easy and straightforward. When you're talking to your partner, aim to listen 80% of the time and only talk 20% of the time. Don't use this technique in every conversation with your partner, as it's not always appropriate and sometimes it's best to keep it at 50/50. Bring it into play only if your partner needs to express something, if you sense an argument coming on, or if you just want to practice being a better listener.

## Measuring Your Happiness with the Magic Relationship Ratio

To better understand relationship happiness, psychologists studied a wide variety of couples by asking them to solve a conflict in 15 minutes. These conversations were taped and watched back nine years later. The same psychologists made predictions about which couples would stay together and which would divorce. Amazingly, a follow-up with the couples involved found that the psychologists were 90% accurate about their predictions!

This led them to their discovery of the Magic Ratio in relationships. They found the major difference between unhappy and happy couples involved the balance of positive and negative interactions during moments of conflict. In this case, a balance of these interactions is not an even split. The Magic Ratio is, in fact, 5:1.

What this means is that for every negative interaction, a healthy and happy couple will have five or more positive interactions to offset the negativity. Negative interactions can include things like eye-rolling, dismissiveness, defensiveness or criticism. And to counteract this, couples should engage in positive interactions like physical affection, well-meaning jokes, apologies, showing appreciation, asking well-intended questions, acceptance, and finding opportunities for agreement. The 5:1 ratio indicates that a couple is happy, healthy, and likely to stay together in the long-run, while a 1:1 ratio is common for couples that are already on the brink of divorce or a break-up.

If there's anything to take away from this ratio, it's that negativity does a great deal of damage! After all, it takes five whole positive interactions just to offset a single negative one. Always keep that in mind moving forward and take care to not let too much negativity seep into your everyday interactions. Think about the last time you were in conflict with your partner. How many instances of positivity and negativity did you both display?

## Stop Freaking Out About these 6 "Problems"

When we get into a deep relationship, so much begins to change – naturally, this makes us worry. Sparks and butterflies are replaced by other feelings, and it isn't entirely clear if this is a good or bad thing. Does this mean you're no longer in love? Is your relationship doomed to fail? Stop worrying! More often than not, couples worry about something that is completely normal.

## Relationship Communication

It's important that we eliminate the habit of freaking out. When we freak out, we are so caught up in the emotion that we don't consider an actual solution. And let me tell you, there *are* solutions. Here are some of the most common relationship problems and better yet, how you can fix them through communication.

### 1. Your relationship isn't as exciting as it used to be

Of all complaints and worries, this one is by far the most common. Ask every single long-term couple and they'll tell you the excitement from their early days has settled. The rush of a new experience has been replaced by a sense of familiarity and closeness. Don't freak out about this! You've found stability. Don't think of it as having lost something, but as entering a new phase. Your relationship has leveled up.

It's important to distinguish between a relationship that feels less exciting and one that has lost *all* excitement. If you're in the second camp, you've got a little more thinking to do. Either you and your partner have sunk too deep into a rigid routine, or you've lost feelings for one another. Chances are, it's just routine. You've stopped taking care of each others' needs for variety, emotional connection, and personal expansion. Consider having a heart-to-heart and scheduling a date night. Make the effort to spice up your routine. It's not as difficult as you think!

### 2. Sometimes you desperately want alone time

It's not just normal to want alone time, it's actually very healthy. It means you and your partner have avoided becoming codependent and this is vital for the health of a relationship. Craving solitude means you still value your independence and this is something to feel proud of, not worried about.

Telling your partner you need some time apart shouldn't be a difficult discussion. Be direct, be casual, and avoid turning it into a serious talk – making it seem overly serious will cause your partner to think they did something wrong. Just say, "I haven't had any time to myself in a while and I've always needed solitude to recharge. Can I see you after the weekend is over?" If your partner is less independent than you are, conclude with a plan for your next meeting, so they have something to look forward to. Learning to ask for time alone is a fantastic habit to pick up when you're entering a relationship. Ideally, both partners should be able to take time apart whenever they need, without worrying about the other person.

### 3. You caught your partner checking out someone else

The first time you catch your partner's eyes wandering elsewhere, it can be very distressing. It's okay to be taken aback, but you should realize this is a completely normal occurrence. Even the most committed partners will find other people attractive. Attraction towards other people says nothing about their feelings towards you. Think of the last time you saw someone you found attractive. It could have been someone who passed you on the street, or perhaps it was an attractive celebrity in a movie. Remember how your eyes were drawn to that person? It was automatic, but not fueled by any real emotion. Our brains are wired to enjoy looking at what we find attractive, but eye-candy is all it is unless we chase it.

If this is a rare occurrence, it's probably not worth bringing up with your partner. This will only make them feel embarrassed and awkward. It may even cause them to feel anxious if they are around someone they find attractive – leading to even more discomfort for everyone! I only recommend bringing it up if your partner does it continuously and in an overt or disrespectful way. If their eyes linger too long, or it causes them to stop paying attention to you, feel free to say, "Could you please not do that? It really bothers me." Be direct and clear. And remember, this is a very common problem.

### 4. You have very different interests

## Relationship Communication

Ask every relationship or marriage coach, and they'll tell you there are some very healthy, happy couples with completely different interests. Sometimes even opposite interests. In some ways, this can be good for a couple. With different interests, it becomes easy to maintain your independence, something that is very good for long-term partners. When a couple has everything in common, they risk spending too much time together, becoming codependent and if they aren't careful, burning out the fire of their relationship. Embrace the fact that you have different interests. Reframe your perspective: you're not too different, you *complement* each other.

If having different interests means you rarely see each other, make sure to schedule at least two days a week where you can partake in the same activity. For example, you could watch a movie at home, go to the cinema, go out to a jazz bar, or a theater performance. You could even choose to learn a new skill together, like pottery or painting. Talk to each other and come to an agreement about a way you can both have fun together.

### 5. Sometimes your partner really annoys you

You know those moments, don't you? You look over at your partner and you wish they'd just shut up. Or you wish they'd just sit still and stop doing what they're doing. On bad days, you might even become irritated by silly things like how loud they're breathing or how they talk.

Believe it or not, this is normal too – as long as it's not persistent. If you find yourself feeling this way for days on end, there's a chance you've either lost feelings for this person or you're spending too much time together. But if it lasts for only a few or several hours, and then you find yourself returning to your feelings of affection, then you have nothing to worry about. You're just in a normal, long-term relationship! During your moments of annoyance, know that it's normal, and resist the urge to say something hurtful.

**6. You don't have sex as much as you used to**

Surveys have shown this worry as being one of the most common. Couples, at nearly every stage, have some level of concern that they aren't having sex as much as they should. Truth is, it's completely normal for sex to become less frequent over time. And it's normal for the frequency of sex to fluctuate, depending on what's happening in each person's life. Once the honeymoon phase is over, a relationship begins to settle, and that's totally okay! This does not mean your partner no longer desires you, and it certainly does not mean feelings have been lost. If you're still worried, then schedule a time when you and your partner can drop everything and focus on getting intimate. And try something new you haven't done before!

# Chapter Four - Love in Every Way

Communication isn't just about what we say in words. Consider the words, "Oh sure, that would be lovely." You can say that with kindness, but you can also say it with sarcasm, or hesitance. The meaning of everything we say can change based on our tone of voice, facial expression, and the pacing of our speech. Everything we do communicates a message.

Whether we're conscious of it or not, our partner is picking up signals from the way we carry ourselves around them. If you're talking to them but keeping your eyes fixed to your phone, this tells them you're not really interested in the conversation. If your words ask them to open up, but your body is turned towards the TV, this makes your words seem insincere. If you're actively trying to be a better communicator, you must make sure everything you're doing matches the message you're trying to send.

In this chapter, we'll focus on the many ways we can show our partners love. I advise embracing as many expressions of love as you can. And you may be surprised what your partner responds most positively to.

## All You Need to Know about Love Languages

Does it sometimes feel like you and your partner are speaking completely different languages? You just might be. Since renowned marriage counselor, Dr. Gary Chapman, identified the five major love languages, it changed the game for millions of relationships. It demystified relationship dynamics, communication, and overall, fueled a greater understanding between partners.

Every single person gives and receives love in a different way. How we do this determines the actions we find loving and the actions we use to express our love for someone else. The way that we naturally communicate love is called our love language. It's common to have more than one, but rarely do we have more than two dominant love languages.

Two partners who are unaware they have different love languages may feel totally confused by one another. They might even feel unloved and unappreciated, unsure of why their attempts to show love have gone unnoticed. To create a smooth exchange of love and appreciation, it is absolutely vital that couples understand their significant other's love language.

## **Verbal Affirmation**

One of the most common love languages is verbal affirmation. This means we use our words to express love and appreciation. People with this love language feel the most loved when someone verbalizes their feelings, pays them compliments, and gives them lots of verbal encouragement. Here are some examples of verbal affirmation:

- If your partner is ready and noticeably trying to look good, say, "Wow, you look fantastic. You're irresistible in this dress."
- If it's a cozy night in and your partner chooses a great movie to watch, say, "You always know just the right movie to pick. You have great taste."
- If your partner does something considerate, say, "This is so wonderful of you. Thank you. I really appreciate that you went through all this trouble for me."

If this is your partner's love language, pay attention to what they say in words. Do not disregard the kind and loving things they say, as this is how they are expressing love for you. Respond to these loving remarks with verbal appreciation.

## **Quality Time**

## Relationship Communication

Another way we communicate love is by giving our loved ones our undivided attention. Those with this primary love language need to feel a sense of togetherness and intimacy. They feel most loved when their partners make time especially for them and give them their complete focus. This isn't just about sitting together and watching a Netflix show, this is about bonding. Vulnerability is a huge plus for people with this love language. Your actions should send the message: "This time is just for you and I. Right now, I want nothing more than to feel close to you."

To communicate love through quality time, all you need to do is schedule a block of time where you can devote all your attention to your partner, and nothing or no one else. This could be a day at the amusement park, a special date night, or a getaway to a romantic place. It could even be as simple as staying in and sharing your days with each other over their favorite wine. Whatever you do, pay attention and listen carefully.

**<u>Physical Touch</u>**

If you're a very physically affectionate person, it's possible that you prefer to give and receive love through physical touch. A lot can be expressed in the way we touch someone. And as humans, we are wired to respond positively to it. If your partner's love language is physical touch, get used to making loving physical contact. To make your partner feel loved, make sure you hold hands, cuddle, kiss, hug, and nuzzle. People with this love language may also enjoy more sexual intercourse than other people, but this is not always the case.

The best part about this love language is that physical contact is so easy. You don't need much creativity or thought to communicate through touch. When you're passing through the room they're in, give them a peck on the cheek or rub their arm gently. When greeting them or saying goodbye, give them a warm embrace.

**<u>Acts of Service</u>**

If actions mean everything to you, it's possible you receive and give love through acts of service. When this is your love language, you feel most loved when your partner does something you want them to do. This is not at all about being a slave to your partner's every whim, it's about being thoughtful and doing something they didn't ask you to do. If this is your partner's love language, you should take some time to really think about what they'd appreciate the most. Make some aspect of their day easier on them. For example, you could cook your partner a meal they enjoy or fix one of their broken belongings. It could even be as simple as plugging in their phone if you see the battery is low. Perform actions that actively take care of your partner.

### **Gift Giving**

If your love language is gift-giving, this doesn't mean you're a materialistic person. A gift is just physical proof that you've been thinking about someone. It doesn't need to be fancy or expensive. In fact, it doesn't need to cost anything at all. It's just about putting your loving thoughts and intentions into securing a physical object. It's not about the gift itself, it's about the thought behind it. Get used to giving gifts if this is your partner's love language. If they love chocolate, get a box or bar on your way home from work. If their favorite flowers are in bloom, pick up just one or a whole bouquet. And make sure to treat gift-giving holidays seriously!

## How to Use Nonverbal Communication to your Advantage

As we established earlier on in the chapter, your partner is paying attention to everything you're saying, even the things you're not saying in words. To get the best outcome from a conversation, or to soothe them when they are feeling tender, follow these simple but effective nonverbal techniques:

## Relationship Communication

- **Touch your partner in a supportive way**

Don't underestimate the power of touch. Putting an arm around your partner or holding their hand while they talk can make them feel much more at ease. A common tactic couples use when trying to come to an agreement is to cuddle or hold each other in some way, as they talk. Affection and touch can make individuals much more likely to cooperate with each other. Please note, however, that you shouldn't touch your partner if they are extremely angry with you – this can come across as inappropriate and make the situation worse.

- **Keep your facial expression neutral or sympathetic**

When you're listening to your partner speak, make sure your facial expression doesn't discourage them from speaking. If you're in a good mood, keep it sympathetic, and if you're not in a good mood, just keep it neutral. Even if we're upset with our partners, it's important that they feel they can speak without being judged. We may not be saying harsh words, but our facial expressions can still communicate an upsetting message.

Consider this scenario as an example: you're sitting with your partner, explaining to them how you feel very ignored when they're constantly on the phone during your date nights. How would you feel if your partner started looking at you with a raised eyebrow? What if they started scowling? What if it looked like they were about to laugh? Chances are you wouldn't want to continue sharing. And there's even a high likelihood you'd start to feel hesitant about sharing in the future. See? Even when we're not speaking, we're sending a message. Soften your features for a better response.

- **Turn your body towards your partner**

When you're speaking to your partner, especially about something serious, don't simply glance sideways at them. Make sure your entire body is angled towards them. When our bodies are turned away from the person we're speaking to, we send the message that we're not really interested in the conversation at hand. We show we're not truly invested. If your partner is upset or you sense they need some TLC, use your body to face them squarely.

- **Adjust the tone and sound of your voice**

It's not always about what you say, it's also about how you say it. Consider, in the moment, what your partner most needs from you. Do they need to just listen and empathize? If so, speak in a softer, more gentle voice. Do they need reassurance? If so, then speak with a firm, confident voice to make them feel secure. To soothe your significant other, speak slowly as a fast voice can come across as being dismissive.

## Less-Known but Powerful Ways to Show Your Partner Love

Showing our significant other love in one or two forms just won't cut it. Why stop there? Whenever you get the chance, take the opportunity to shower them in warmth and positivity. This isn't just limited to the methods I've listed so far. The ways we can engage in loving behavior are endless.

1. **Publicly declare how proud you are of them**

It doesn't matter who you say it to; when an appropriate time comes up, why don't you proudly share one of your partner's achievements? It doesn't have to be a huge accomplishment, it can be anything that they worked hard on. Recognize your partner's efforts and share their achievement with an outside party. Everyone is taught to stay humble and never brag about their successes, but sometimes we secretly want people to know we succeeded at something. Be the first to share something amazing your partner did. It'll make them feel extremely loved, supported, and they'll likely feel encouraged to keep making progress. This tactic might make them blush at first, but once the shyness wears off, they'll feel very touched.

## 2. Stand up for your significant other

If something unfair happens to your partner, don't be afraid of speaking up. This doesn't mean you should start a fight or say something nasty, it simply means you should vocalize your support during a difficult situation. Use your common sense to determine the right way to do this. If you're in a conversation with lots of people and someone puts your partner down, counter it by acting as their cheerleader.

Consider this example: Adam and Vanessa are out with a group of friends. Someone starts making fun of Vanessa because she mentioned she was writing a novel. The rude person remarks on how everyone else is working a high-paying corporate job while Vanessa is at home writing stories. Adam doesn't need to start a fight to stand up for her. All he says is, "Writing a novel takes a lot of patience and determination. Vanessa has been working very hard and I think it's wonderful that she's chasing her passion instead of becoming money-obsessed." No negativity required!

## 3. Make an effort to bond with the people close to them

It's true what they say; when you start dating someone, you date their close friends and family as well. Whether you like it or not, these people are here to stay. And if you don't make the effort to leave a positive impression, their opinions could have an influence on the course of your relationship. When you get to know your partner's close connections, you send the message that you really want to be a part of your loved one's life. You demonstrate you're serious, and you display genuine love. Why? Because you're engaging in an entirely unselfish pursuit. After all, your partner's friends and family don't satisfy any of your needs and desires. Don't give in to the idea that they aren't important because they're not your partner. How you treat them speaks volumes about how you see your relationship.

### 4. Ask your partner what they enjoy in the bedroom

There's this unhealthy idea that we should all just *know* what our partners want, without ever asking them. Many people are under the mistaken impression that if we can't just figure it out on our own, we're not good in bed. This is a ridiculous notion. We're not mind-readers and every single person has different preferences. A lot of people are not forthcoming about what they like because they don't want to seem demanding, so why not just ask? How can we get it right if we never know?

Even if you already know what your partner likes, there's nothing wrong with having a check-in. Ask them if there's anything you did recently that they enjoyed, and ask them if there's anything you can do better. Learning to communicate openly about sex is one of the best things we can do in our relationships. It also shows our partner how devoted we are to making them happy and meeting their needs. Even if we don't always get it right, it can make the difference to know we're trying.

### 5. Learn more about a topic that interests them

If your partner is a huge science-fiction nerd, try and watch their favorite show or movie. If they love discussing politics but you don't understand it, ask them to explain something to you. Open up and expand your horizons! Show your partner you're really interested in what they care about. You never know, you may even find that you're interested in it as well. We should always try to create opportunities for bonding with our partner. By engaging with what interests them, we create more intimate moments. This is a sure way to strengthen your connection.

## 6. Take care of them when they're sick

It's fairly common for women to take on a nurturing role when their partners are sick, but unfortunately it's less common to see it happen the other way around. One of the most loving things we can do for our partners is to take care of them when they're at their weakest. This includes all types of physical and mental ailments, including sickness, depression, or even grief. This doesn't mean we have to wait on them hand and foot; it just means offering some strength when they need it the most. This loving gesture tells our partner that we care for them, even when they are too weak to offer us anything in return.

## 7. Make time to relive your love story

Every single couple has a unique love story. It encompasses all the wonderful, exciting things about a new romance: how you met, what you first thought of each other, when you knew you wanted to be with them, and so much more. A great way to continue reigniting love and passion is by actively reliving your love story with your partner. Why not revisit the place you had your first date? Or the place you had your first kiss? Or how about just tell each other your different sides of the story? When did you both know it was love? When a couple does this, they're taking a step back to remember why they're with each other. They are disconnecting from their current troubles and making the effort to not lose sight of the magic. We all have a love story; take the time to remember yours.

## 8. Make plans for the future

Alright, calm down, this doesn't mean you need to start planning your wedding or naming your future children. It just means you need to paint a future with your partner in it. It's not about committing to forever, it's about coming up with shared goals and creating shared dreams. Identify something you can both work towards achieving together. This creates a more hopeful and collaborative environment in the relationship. By doing this, we show our partner that they, too, are part of the dream and part of the goal. It is the positive kind of self-fulfilling prophecy, where we subconsciously do our best to thrive alongside our partner because we have a goal to reach for.

# Chapter Five - Decoding Your Partner

In the early days of a romance, getting to know the person you're madly attracted to is an exciting pursuit. Everything about them is fascinating and almost spellbinding. Every new quirk you discover is adorable, even the objectively annoying ones. Their unique qualities draw you in and you're convinced there's no one like them in the world. Your feelings are on fire in the best way possible. You can't wait to fully unravel your partner and deeply get to know them in every single way.

Once things become serious, your attitude is likely to see a shift. This isn't a bad thing. In fact, it's extremely normal, as I've demonstrated in the first chapter. While you still love your partner and their unique quirks, you've also discovered the other dimensions to their personality, the sides that weren't apparent in the early days at all. Every person has a dark side. We all have inner conflicts, our own particular needs, and even when all our secrets are laid bare, there are bad days where we suddenly play to an entirely different tune. Like I mentioned, this is completely normal. This is human nature. This will happen in every relationship you encounter and to be a good partner, you need to learn to roll with it.

Your significant other may feel like a mystery at times, but he or she is far more simple than you think. It all comes down to the basic needs which we all share, and some unique needs which are entirely their own. You'll learn about them over time and gradually perfect how to take care of them. The process of decoding your partner takes awareness, understanding, and kindness, but it's one of the best things you can do for your relationship. This is what love is all about.

## Understanding Your Partner's Particular Needs

With every single partner you're with, you're going to need to take the temperature on their various needs. Trouble is, 'needs' is such a vague term, and you may not be sure where to begin. If you want to make your partner happy, consider these different types of needs and make sure you understand your partner's preferences. This may take some intent observation, but you should also feel free to just openly discuss these topics with your partner. This way, there is no confusion at all.

- **Their sex drive and sexual needs**

It's true that our sex drives can fluctuate but some people just have a much higher sex drive than others, at all times. And there are also other people that just don't crave it as much. Assess your partner's needs or just straight-up ask your partner how high they would rate their sex drive. You may find they have a similar sex drive to you, but you may also find you have differing needs. This means that later on you'll need to find a compromise so neither partner feels unsatisfied. You'll also need to discover what they specifically enjoy in the bedroom. Keep in mind that everyone's different and it may even be beneficial to just outright ask your partner what they like.

- **The way they destress and relax**

There are certainly common threads, but for the most part, we all have different ways of destressing and unwinding. For some people, this can mean total peace and quiet, eating healthy food, and taking a walk in the park. At the opposite extreme, some people like watching loud TV, playing video games, and want nothing more than to gorge on greasy pizza. You'll even find that some people like to be social when they relax, and others like to be completely alone. It's always best to find out what your partner's needs are after a long day. Once you know, you can help create the right environment for them when you know they need it the most. It's also perfectly normal for people to have a few ways they like to destress, but you'll likely notice a pattern. If you and your partner have conflicting ways of destressing, make sure to find a way to compromise.

- **Their idea of adventure**

Adventure doesn't always mean skydiving or roller-coasters; our need for adventure arises when we have energy and are in the mood to do something fun. Maybe even something different from our usual routine. We're ready to exert energy, instead of trying to preserve it. A common idea of adventure in the modern day is going out for a night on the town, dancing, and having some delicious cocktails. But some people, even on their best days, don't want to do this at all. Some people like to be indoors and engaging in private activities. Perhaps, they want to cook or bake, or do a home work-out video. When it comes to adventure, we're much more likely to have many ideas of fun. In this case, it's best to note what your partner's favorite thing is, and to rule out what they definitely *do not* consider fun. It's important that whatever they like to do, you either learn to enjoy it too or just accept that they enjoy doing it.

- **Their needs for mental and intellectual stimulation**

To put it simply, what we find mentally and intellectually stimulating is what we find interesting. It encompasses all the topics that we enjoy feeling challenged by and exploring. This is one of the easiest needs to discover as people are more upfront about what mentally stimulates them. You just need to pay attention.

Some people choose to not classify this as a need, but I would beg to differ. When we are deprived of what we find interesting, our personalities wilt and we feel lackluster, perhaps even depressed. Those who stop engaging with topics they enjoy can even complain of feeling less like themselves. It's important, once we identify these stimulation needs in our partner, to always actively listen and participate as much as we can. What are the topics that bring your partner joy? When do you see their eyes come alive? Whatever these topics are, we must always allow our partner to bring them into the wider conversation. This is how we can help satisfy their need for personal expansion.

- **Their emotional support needs**

Inevitably, a time will arise when your partner needs emotional support. While their needs will vary with each circumstance, you'll notice there are patterns in what they find soothing during times of emotional hardship. For some people, it's important to cry, in which case you should make sure to be an understanding shoulder to cry on. Some people become more hungry and have more cravings during times of emotional stress, in which case, you should try to give them whatever food they find nourishing. There are even people who need to be completely alone to feel supported. They may just want to escape into nature by themselves and they'll need you to understand that. Whenever your partner is going through a time of hurt, try to learn what eases the pain. During these periods, it can also be a good idea to turn to the five love languages.

- **Their spiritual or religious needs**

If your partner doesn't adhere to any specific spiritual or religious practice, then there's no need to worry about this section. However, more often than not, we encounter people that have some shred of spirituality in their lives. Spirituality and religion is a highly personal matter, and it's highly important that we respect our partner's choices and beliefs. Even if it seems silly to us, it brings our partner peace and this is all that matters. Know what your partner's spiritual practices are, when they need to do it, and if there are any other requirements they need to abide by, such as dietary restrictions. We should never argue with their spiritual needs and we should never make fun of them.

- **Their insecurities and needs for reassurance**

You're never going to find a partner without any insecurities. That's just how it is. We're all human and we all have fears shaped by our backgrounds or personalities. It is absolutely vital that you understand what your partner's insecurities are. And most importantly, you must know how to prevent bringing those insecurities to the surface, and what they need from you when they do arise. For example, let's say your partner is insecure about his or her weight. This insecurity might be triggered when they meet someone very thin and attractive. These situations are unavoidable so it's best to come up with an action-plan for when it does happen. Perhaps, later on, you should try and tell your partner how sexy they are, and focus all your energy on making them feel attractive. Or perhaps, your partner would prefer to just forget it and do something that takes their mind off their body entirely. These needs will differ from person-to-person.

# 5 Absolutely Essential Things to Do When Your Partner Has Experienced Trauma

When you finally meet the person you want to be with, chances are they saw a heck of a lot before you came along. Sometimes even, a little too much. If your partner has been touched by trauma in their romantic or sexual encounters, you'll have to be more gentle with them. This is a non-negotiable. If we don't adjust our behavior, we will never make our partners happy, and we may end up causing more damage.

There are many types of trauma that can leave a painful and emotional scar, from cheating to emotional abuse, and in some cases, more physical kinds of abuse. Communication tactics should always be softened during specific scenarios to ensure you don't trigger them or cause them to withdraw. Always keep the following tips in mind if your partner has endured trauma:

1. **Learn about the trauma in a non-intrusive manner**

Before we know what to do, we must know what we are dealing with. The first step is to try and learn about the traumatic incident. Depending on the severity of the trauma, it may not be as simple as asking our partner what happened. If it is too painful to recount or they are just not ready to tell us, there are only two things we can do: wait for them to feel ready, or ask someone they are close to. A good first action is to tell your partner, "You don't have to tell me anything you don't want to, but I'm always here if you want to share. I just want to know how I can support you in the best way possible." Let them know you care about their past, are ready to listen, but that you won't push them to do anything they don't want to do. It's important that you never force or guilt-trip them in this situation.

2. **Consider the types of behavior that may trigger their traumatic memories**

This stage requires your deep thought. Think of the qualities and behavior that hurt them during this traumatic incident. Sometimes it's straightforward, such as physical violence, but not all the time. If your partner was cheated on, they may feel triggered by something as mild as you talking to members of the opposite sex. They may become anxious on the nights you go out drinking with your friends. If there are moments where you stop communicating, this could be especially hard for them as they might suspect you are keeping a secret. Identify the behavior involved in the traumatic incident, but also what may have led to it.

## 3. Decide on alternative or modified ways of behaving

It's not always realistic to eliminate every single behavior that could possibly trigger our partner. While it's easy (and absolutely necessary) to not abuse someone, it's not easy or realistic to completely stop talking to members of the opposite sex. So what can we do instead? It's simple: we must modify the way we engage in this behavior. For example, if you're texting a member of the opposite sex, you could consider letting your partner see the messages so they can ease their worries. If they become anxious when you're out drinking with buddies, consider having a check-in via phone call every couple of hours. Or send them a photo of you at your current location. Get creative about how you can modify your behavior without eliminating completely normal actions. And you should always feel free to simply ask your partner, "What can I do to make you feel better in this situation?"

## 4. Understand what they need if they are triggered

Hopefully this never happens, but if your partner's trauma is linked to common events, it may be inevitable. When this happens, you must be completely calm and gentle with your partner. If you are angry with them for some reason, you must put this on hold until they've stopped feeling overwhelmed. Otherwise, this will only exacerbate the situation.

How this situation manifests will vary with each person, but the most common response is either crying or going into self-defense mode, as if the trauma is happening again and they must protect themselves. The best thing to do is to offer reassurance and take on a soothing tone of voice. If your partner was a victim of violence, play it safe and do not touch them at all until they are ready. Understand that sometimes our partners may not have obvious signs of being triggered. Instead, they may just become quiet and depressed. It's important to keep an eye out for less noticeable responses if you know they've been exposed to a potential trigger.

What each person needs depends highly on the person and the trauma they experienced. A good rule of thumb is to remove the trigger as soon as possible and do the opposite of what started it.

**5. Know what you can do to help them move on**

If the trauma is severe and very rarely comes up, then it's best to disregard this stage entirely. However, if the trauma is getting in the way of your relationship, or preventing your partner from advancing their life, think of ways to help them make more peace with what happened. This could mean seeking out professional help or coming up with step-by-step solutions amongst yourselves. It's important that these solutions are not just your responsibility; these steps should also challenge your partner to create more healthy response patterns.

Let's go back to the example of the jealous partner. It's not realistic to expect someone to call you every couple of hours every single time they go out drinking. Ideally, the jealous partner should move on from this behavior once the relationship starts to become more long-term. To start this positive transition, they could make calls less frequent during each night out, or they could decide to just text every hour. The jealous partner should come up with steps they can do to avoid feeling low or depressed during these incidents. Perhaps, they could also go out with friends or channel their energy into an intense work-out session. Create a positive new habit to take the place of unhealthy responses. This way, everyone wins.

# Chapter Six - It's All About You

We're often told we should find a significant other that loves us as we are. This is true, to an extent. We should all expect our partners to love and accept us for our likes, dislikes, and our positive attributes without trying to change them. They should even love us for our quirks, flaws, and idiosyncrasies. They should love what makes us different. But no partner should ever be expected to put up with negative or destructive behavior that deeply affects them. Your arrogant attitude, your manipulative tendencies, your persistent laziness; none of this is your partner's responsibility and if it hurts them, you'd be cruel to ask them to accept it. Asking our partners to deal with what upsets them and hurts them will inevitably lead to contempt. And contempt is one of the few things a relationship cannot heal from.

The majority of relationships fail because one or both partners refuse to do the self-work. I urge you now to not be the partner that doesn't do the self-work. Don't be the one who doesn't make the effort. You may feel indignant now, but if the relationship ends and you know you didn't try your hardest, you're going to be left drowning in regret. Work on you, before it's too late.

And remember, it doesn't end here. The behavior that hurts your partner now will likely hurt all your future partners to come. As long as you want to be in a happy, healthy relationship, you will continue to need positive self-transformation.

## How to Instantly Become a Better Partner

If you want to do right by your partner, implement these easy habits into your dynamic. Create these new communication norms and you'll instantly start to see better results in your relationship.

## Relationship Communication

### 1. Ask for what you need

Stop expecting your significant other to read your mind. They have their own life, with their own needs, and you can't expect them to sit around trying to guess how you feel. Asking for what you need does not make you needy, it makes you self-aware and emotionally mature. It shows you value your relationship because you're serious about creating better conditions. Instead of expecting your partner to jump through hoops, you are being upfront about how to help. This makes it easy on them. This gives them a real opportunity to adjust their behavior.

When you ask for what you need, you are much more likely to *get* what you need. To get the best outcome from your discussion, remember to use "I feel" statements.

### 2. Bring up a problem before it gets worse

There are many reasons we avoid bringing up problems. Sometimes it's because we're uncomfortable with confrontation, afraid of the other person's response, or perhaps, we just don't want to admit there's a problem. What usually happens is the problem continues and gets worse. When we avoid bringing up our problems, we risk two things.

- Exploding at our partner when we just can't take it anymore. When we allow ourselves to reach our breaking point, we are more likely to say something harsh that we don't mean. This can upset our significant other and it may even cause lasting damage to the relationship.

- Developing contempt for our partner. If we don't give our partner the opportunity to make it better, it will not get better. This will frustrate us more and more, and eventually lead to resentment. You may find your mind swarming with questions like, "How on earth can he/she not notice? Why isn't he/she more aware of what this is doing to me?" This can spiral into feelings of not feeling cared for, and anger at your partner for putting you through this. Newsflash: you are putting *yourself* through this if you don't tell your partner what's wrong!

### 3. Pay attention to timing

Always consider the timing of what you do and say to your partner. This makes a massive difference in the response you receive from them. If you're trying to have a serious talk with them, don't do it when they're exhausted from work or if they've had a bad day. This could incite an argument since they're not in their right mind. Always use timing to your advantage. Talk to your partner the morning after they've had a night of great sleep or on a day they seem level-headed.

This rule extends even beyond serious talks and discussions. Whenever you're going to make any decision that impacts both you and your partner, think of where this will fall on their timeline and schedule. If there are days of the year that are particularly hard for your partner (for example, anniversaries of deaths), remember them. Ensure you don't plan any big social events when they would prefer to lay low.

### 4. Use gentle and constructive language

Mistakes happen. And sometimes our partners don't always have the greatest ideas. Still, you should always make the effort to stay constructive when providing your partner with any feedback. Acknowledge what they did right, but also point out opportunities for growth. If you feel the need to criticize your partner, always reframe your comments from the perspective of how they can improve. If you make them feel like everything they do is wrong, you're not fixing the situation, and you're only disempowering them from cooperating with you. Always focus on solutions.

### 5. Always listen, always

This one gets repeated a lot, but it's for a good reason. Active listening in our relationship is extremely important. In fact, it is directly linked to the overall quality of communication with our partner. And in an unhappy couple, it is highly common for at least one partner to complain that they don't feel heard and their significant other never listens to them. By listening, we are staying present in the conversation. We are showing our partner respect. And by actively listening, we are also lowering the likelihood of misunderstandings. The next time your partner is speaking, avoid just waiting for your turn to reply and really absorb everything they're saying.

### 6. Keep your expectations kind and realistic

We all move through life and make progress at different paces. This is no more true for you and your partner. One way you can cause needless disappointment for yourself and hurt for your partner is by expecting far too much from them. If it seems like you're always waiting for your partner to tick off boxes on your checklist, take a step back and re-examine the extent of what you're asking. If you find yourself continuously disappointed, consider why before taking any further action. Are you trying to change their personality? Are you asking for too big of an adjustment too fast? Are your demands being insensitive to their current life circumstances? These are all necessary questions to ask yourself.

Some specific examples of unfair expectations:

- Expecting your partner to be on top of all the chores when someone close to them has just passed away.

## Relationship Communication

- Wanting your partner to become athletic because you are most attracted to athletic people.
- Expecting your partner to cook a wonderful meal and keep the house spotless after a stressful day at work.
- Demanding that your partner immediately become great at that move you like in bed, when they're already giving it their best effort.
- Expecting your partner to have all the same positive qualities as your previous partner.

Please note that these expectations do not apply to matters of compassion, respect, safety, consideration, and kindness. These do not count as high expectations, this is basic human decency. No matter what your partner is going through, they should always be meeting these basic expectations.

### 7. Stop bringing up the past

To clarify, it's not bringing up the past in itself that's damaging, it's when we dredge up the past to start an argument. If you've already talked about it and your partner has apologized, we shouldn't continue to hold their mistakes against them. If we do this, we're demonstrating we haven't truly forgiven them. As long as we continue to hold this grudge, we are creating negativity in the relationship. Either you should move past this mistake and forgive your partner, or if you can't forgive them, do what needs to be done and end the relationship. Continuing to throw past mistakes in our partner's face is a cruel act as it traps them in the mistake. Not only this, but it increases the likelihood of us getting into circuitous conversations that are never solved. Since we are so attached to the problem, we can never move onto solutions. Stop using the past as a weapon and try your best to move on, if you're deciding to stay.

### 8. Express gratitude more often

Science has proven that when we approach life with gratitude, we instantly feel happier. Not only does expressing gratitude in our relationships lead to our own happy feelings, but it can be transformative and powerful for our partners. By showing gratitude, we are reminding them of their tremendous worth and highlighting what they are doing right.

Being on the receiving end of gratitude can be incredibly empowering. If your partner is going through a hard time, it will ignite more motivation and progress, ultimately creating more satisfaction in the long run. But most importantly, it shows them that their efforts do not go unseen and that you recognize all they do. This will instantly make them feel more positive and valued. Gratitude is, overall, a big win for everyone. Express it more often! You'll be glad you did. It's as simple as telling your partner "I love you and appreciate you" or highlighting a specific action they did/do and explaining in more detail why you're so grateful for it.

## Understanding Your Relationship Attachment Style

Our attachment styles are formed in early childhood and they play a major role in our relationships. According to psychoanalysts, the attachment style we form all comes down to the dynamic we had with our caregivers, during infancy. This style determines our behavior patterns, the types of relationships we're most likely to choose, and essentially how we go about getting our needs met.

No attachment style is 'bad' per se, but some are less conducive to harmonious relationships and more inclined to exhibit unhealthy behavior. In any case, it's always important that we're aware of our attachment style (and our partner's as well) so we can have a better understanding of our behavior patterns and responses.

- **The Anxious-Preoccupied Attachment Style**

Those with this style tend to crave emotional attachment and may have a history of tumultuous relationships. They tend to dislike being alone and are prone to fantasizing about their dream partner. Unfortunately, this attachment style encounters a lot of stressors in a relationship. A lot of these are self-inflicted. During times of emotional distress, they can become jealous, possessive, or needy. They require a lot of love and validation, and they may react negatively if they don't receive reassurance or positive reinforcement.

It can be said that these types live in their heads a lot. They are often their own worst enemy, intensely worried they'll be betrayed. Those with this attachment style make up about 20% of the population.

- **The Dismissive-Avoidant Attachment Style**

Quite the opposite of the Anxious type, the Dismissive-Avoidant is highly self-sufficient. This type displays a great amount of independence and requires a lot of freedom in their relationships. Though they may secretly desire a deep connection, they will appear closed-off and rarely engage deeply in relationships. Many people who date these types end up complaining that they seem emotionally unavailable and at times, even indifferent. It takes more work for them to show vulnerability, and some may even be commitment-phobic. They tend to see intimacy as a loss of their personal freedom.

Avoidant types are so accustomed to taking care of their own needs that they can become plagued by obsessions as a way to self-medicate. This may be substance abuse, or something less damaging like exercise or food. Roughly 23% of the population consists of these types.

- **The Fearful-Avoidant Attachment Style**

This type lives with a lot of conflict. A combination of the previous two styles, the Fearful-Avoidant exhibits a push-pull pattern of behavior. They deeply crave a close connection and yet part of them wants to run away to safety. Unfortunately, this type tends to do both those things. During their worst moments, they may cling to their partner and even appear quite needy. But once their partner gets close to them and comforts them, they may suddenly feel suffocated and trapped. Like Anxious types, the Fearful personalities are also prone to turbulent relationships.

These unpredictable types don't have a fixed strategy for meeting their needs. Their behavior patterns are often a result of trauma from abandonment or abuse. This is the most rare attachment style, making up only 1% of the population.

- **The Secure Attachment Style**

As its name suggests, this attachment style is the most secure of the four, and is widely considered the most emotionally healthy. They have higher levels of emotional intelligence and find it easier to regulate their emotions. Healthy boundaries are easy to set and they have a generally positive outlook on relationships. This type feels secure in a relationship, and they also do just fine on their own. Overall, they tend to be more satisfied in relationships and have a much easier time forming a healthy connection.

The Secure Attachment style is formed when one's childhood is experienced as mostly positive. Caregivers were perceived as secure and safe, so they continue to project this experience onto all future relationships. This is the most common type of all, with 57% of the population characterized as Secure.

Most people don't change their attachment styles, but it is entirely possible to do so. Any individual with one of the less-healthy styles can develop more secure qualities with tremendous self-work. In order for this to happen, however, the individual must pursue therapy and/or seek out the companionship of someone with a secure attachment style. By cultivating self-awareness and a willingness to develop better habits, anyone can transition out of their unhealthy behavior.

## Must-Know Tips for Starting a New Relationship When You Have a History of Bad Relationships

Do you have one of the first three attachment styles? If so, you've probably had a few bad relationships, maybe even abusive relationships. You may be working through some negative or even outright destructive behavior, but rest assured, it is possible to move on. Plenty of people have done it on their own. And with a loving companion by your side, you can work on it together.

The trauma we endure can shape the way we communicate with our partners and the imagined stressors we're more likely to experience. For this reason, we may express more fear, anger, or distress in situations that would not normally upset someone. This isn't always fair on our partners, especially since they aren't the ones that hurt us, and it's important we don't become abusive ourselves or cause our new partners pain. Keep the following tips in mind to maintain your emotional and mental health, while also being considerate of your partner.

*Please note that if your trauma is severe, these tips are not meant to substitute for help from a mental health professional.*

1. **Make a list of behavior you will no longer tolerate**

## Relationship Communication

In order to turn over a new leaf successfully, it's essential that we identify what we wish to remove from our lives. If you've had a history of experiencing pain, make a list of behavior in previous partners that caused you significant pain. This list is exactly what you should no longer tolerate in relationships from now on. There's no way to make excuses for future abusive partners because this list makes it simple; they either did it or they didn't. Refer back to it to remind yourself of its contents and feel free to show it to new partners once you're seriously dating.

Having this list is also helpful because during times of emotional distress, our feelings can cloud our judgment. It can save us from directing unwarranted anger or upset at partners who didn't do anything wrong. For example, if you're having a bad day, you may feel more suspicious or anxious than usual. If your partner does something, you may overreact. Looking back at your list, you'll see that your partner didn't actually exhibit the behavior you outlined. This will make it clear that the feeling likely comes from within, because you're having a bad day.

For this list to be truly successful, we should strictly write down behavior and not emotions. Adding to your list that you will not tolerate anyone causing you pain makes things tricky; sometimes we can impose pain on ourselves and mistakenly believe it is the fault of our partners. And feel free to get an outside opinion on whether the behavior noted down is sufficient and reasonable.

### 2. When you're ready, share what happened with your new partner

In order for our partners to support us in the best way possible, they need to know what they're dealing with. Without knowledge of what happened and how it affected us, they'll have no clue how to help. Share with them what happened, what you need from them, and what you're doing to help yourself move on.

If you're not ready to tell them just yet, then wait till you're ready, but in the meantime, don't expect them to just *know* how to help. If you don't think you'll be ready to share with them any time soon, feel free to ask a friend to tell your new partner. Although this isn't the ideal way of letting them know, it is better than leaving them in the dark. All in all, it's always best for your new partner to have as much information as possible so they can offer the exact support you need.

### 3. Rely on your support system whenever necessary

Our closest friends and family are our greatest allies. If you're ever unsure, use them as your sounding board and ask them for an outside opinion. Our feelings are not always trustworthy since past trauma makes us more predisposed to feel a certain way. Ask someone you trust who can give you a neutral opinion. Don't make all the big decisions on your own.

Furthermore, it's also essential that the person you're relying on for advice is someone whose love life you seek to emulate. Opinions are not all made equal. If a person in a healthy relationship gives you one piece of advice, but ten people in bad relationships say the opposite, you should always listen to the person who has lived the outcome you most desire. Look for the most neutral people possible; if you struggle with jealousy, don't get advice from someone who also struggles with jealousy.

### 4. Resist making comparisons to previous partners

When we're in a new relationship, it is completely natural for our brains to use past relationships and partners as reference points. This is just what the brain does to try and understand a new situation. Although the instinct is natural, keep in mind that its analyses are not always correct. When we encounter new territory, our past experiences are a highly limited pool of knowledge to extrapolate from.

Make the effort to remind yourself that your current partner is not your previous partner. Your brain will try to make comparisons, but resist them when you can. If the attitude your new partner exhibits is different to what you previously experienced, then remind yourself there's no reason to expect the same outcome. If there's no real evidence, there's no reason to believe the worst. If your previous partner cheated on you with a friend of the opposite sex, remember that there are many individuals who don't do this. There's no reason to become angry or upset right off-the-bat. Your current partner did not hurt you like your previous partner, so do not punish them for something they didn't do.

It is especially important that we don't vocalize any comparisons to previous partners. If our current partner did nothing wrong, this will come across as very insulting. If you get the urge to do this in the heat of the moment, resist it at all costs.

### 5. Do not expect your partner to fix everything for you

You should definitely expect support from your partner during times of healing. However, there's a big difference between support and an emotional or psychological crutch. Support crosses the line into 'crutch' territory when you stop doing things for yourself. Instead of doing the self-work to transform your behavior and thinking patterns, you expect your partner to change *their* behavior. There is suddenly intense pressure on the 'crutch' partner to fix everything and if anything goes wrong, it automatically becomes their fault. Avoid this dynamic at all costs! This is a sure way to get your partner to resent you and no one would blame them – forcing someone to be your crutch is cruel!

When we engage in dynamics like this, we immediately become stagnant. Since someone else is babying us, we are never challenged, and this means we won't grow. Remember that feeling uncomfortable isn't always bad. We should always examine our discomforts and see if it's something we can work on, before asking someone to change. Don't expect your partner to meet all your needs (and more!) without meeting any of theirs in return. A history of bad relationships is not a good excuse to take advantage of a new partner.

## 6. Start making self-care an essential part of your routine

One powerful thing we can do for ourselves is engage in self-care practices. Ditch the idea that self-care is only for special occasions and incorporate it into your daily or weekly routine. Self-care does not have to cost any money; it just means you're allowing yourself to do whatever it is that makes you feel calm and taken care of. You know it's self-care when you reconnect to who you are and when you feel at peace. This can mean taking a warm bubble bath and listening to your favorite music. Or this can mean going to a relaxing cafe, journaling, and reading a great book or treating yourself to some baked goods. If you've got a bigger budget, you can get a massage and indulge in chocolate. The possibilities are endless!

When we start making self-care part of our routine, we also rewire our brain to feel its effects more often. It's not just the bubble bath or massage that becomes the new norm, the peace and calm becomes more of a norm as well. This is essential when we're recovering from trauma because we are in deep need of rewiring responses and impulses. In addition to this, however, it is a powerful symbol for the new chapter you will begin. By carving out time to focus on you, you are vowing to start thinking of your needs more often. You are recognizing your importance and you are saying no to relationships that cause you pain. Self-care for the win.

# Chapter Seven - The Ticking Time Bomb

When we're considering potential partners, we tend to put too much weight in excitement and passion. While that's, no doubt, extremely important, we neglect what really makes the meat of a relationship. Almost anyone can bring a fun time to the table, but what will they do during the hard times? The dark nights when an argument goes round in circles? When voices are raised and it feels like your blood is boiling? The way you and your partner behave and react in these situations has the biggest bearing on your relationship. Your sex life and the number of interests you have in common: neither of these factors are a true test of your strength as a team. The biggest signifier of your relationship's strength is how you fight and how you find solutions to problems.

Even if you're soulmates and you have a blast together every single day, there are going to be days and nights where you can't stand each other. While no one is perfect at the beginning of a relationship, it is essential that we learn over time. There will come a time when we need to handle a ticking time bomb (a highly sensitive situation) and in order to prevent it from exploding, the necessary knowledge and tools are required. Expect that challenges will arise and be prepared to solve them.

## When to Press the Pause or Stop Button

Open communication can solve many problems, but there are times when you need to take a step back. Talking doesn't always make things better, sometimes it can cause damage and needless distress. If it's an important discussion, then press the pause button and resume the talk when both parties are more level-headed. If the conversation isn't about anything important, press stop and drop the topic like a hot potato. These are the signs you need to cool off and let it sit:

## Relationship Communication

- **Emotions are running high**

If there are tears, raised voices, and you get the distinct feeling someone (and this includes you) might explode, press that pause button. When emotions get too charged and intense, there's a higher likelihood of someone boiling over and saying something hurtful. You may even make a decision you can't take back. To press pause successfully, say something like:

"I sense we're both getting too consumed by our emotions. Why don't we settle down and resume this conversation later? I want to solve this problem and in our current state, I don't think we can."

Once both parties have had a chance to cool off, you'll come back more rational and level-headed. A potential disaster will have been averted and you'll feel grateful for taking that break.

- **You've had this conversation before and it didn't end well**

For many couples, there can be recurring discussions that never seem to get solved. Some of these can bring out the worst in both partners and end in bitter, hurtful remarks that do a lot of damage. If you find this dead-end discussion cropping up again, nip it in the bud while you can. Consider saying:

"The last time we had this talk, we both said a lot of things we didn't mean. I feel that it did more harm than good, and I really don't want to see that situation repeated. I really want to fix this situation so how about we take some time to think about solutions? We can each think of ways to move forward. And we can resume this discussion when we have new ideas to bring to the table."

If the discussion has no bearing on the relationship, simply point out what happened last time, and say you feel it's best to agree to disagree. Each couple will have their own versions of dead-end topics, and you need to learn when it's not important to win.

- **At least one partner is tired**

When we're tired, we can sometimes lose the energy required to regulate ourselves and our emotions. That's not to say the emotions we feel when we are tired aren't real. In fact, oftentimes this can display what we really feel – but we become less able to deal with them maturely and effectively. When we have energy, our brain can easily go through the process of organizing our words and thoughts in a clear, constructive manner. When we don't have energy, our brains can fail to get this process started or do it properly.

When we enter an argument in this tired state, we are not using the best tools we have. We are not equipped to be in the arena and it's best we get out before we cause damage. In this state of mind, we are much more likely to overreact and say something we don't mean. We shouldn't always expect our partners to understand that we're just tired and move on. If what we say is genuinely hurtful, it can cause deep hurt. Do not get into serious talks with your partner when one partner cannot communicate effectively in that moment.

- **Words have started to get hurtful**

For one reason or another, a conversation can really start to sour. You'll know this is starting to happen because either your partner will say something that stings or you'll say something you normally wouldn't say. If you notice that tone and language are starting to get aggressive or mean, then you need to walk away immediately and cool off. This is the point in our arguments that we should always try to avoid. Our heated conversations should never hurt. And if it does, know that it has gone too far.

Don't just walk out without saying a word, as this will appear as storming off, which could only further anger your partner. Instead, point out to your partner that you've started to say things you don't mean, and emphasize that you don't want to co-create a situation that does lasting damage. Suggest that you both take time to calm down and think about more constructive ways of getting your points across.

- **The conversation is going around in circles**

This often happens when both partners are tired, especially when they've exhausted themselves by having such a drawn-out argument. You'll notice that the same points continue to be raised, the same responses made each time, and yet somehow you keep coming back to the same thing over and over.

This is a sign your conversation has gone around in circles. If someone doesn't end it soon, it will only continue to go on and on, and a solution will likely never be found. Try to point out the conversation has become circuitous as soon as you notice. It could end with hurtful statements made, but even if it doesn't, it's a huge waste of time and energy for both partners.

If you find a certain topic leads you around in circles a lot, consider having this conversation via email. When discussions are written out, it's much easier to see where the confusion lies. By examining the responses closely, it becomes clear why the discussion always becomes circuitous.

- **The outcome of the discussion won't actually affect the relationship**

If the conversation is getting heated, consider whether the topic actually matters. Let's say you've both started to argue about a topic on the news. Ask yourself what difference it makes if you both agree or disagree. Does disagreeing on this topic make you have less fun together? Does it hurt you in any way? Does it affect either of your abilities to be good partners for one another? If the answer is 'no' to all of these questions, then this topic is not that important. The outcome does not affect your relationship in any way – so don't rile yourselves up over nothing.

## How to Bring Up Your Concerns the Right Way

If you're going to be in a happy, healthy relationship, you need to know how to raise your concerns the right way. In other words, without causing significant damage to your partner and while being honest enough to incite change. These are incredibly sensitive situations, so pay close attention to the following tips:

- **Choose timing carefully**

Remember what we said about paying attention to timing? That's even more important when we're about to have a big talk. Don't bring up serious conversations when your partner is having a bad day or when they are exhausted. This will not lead to a favorable outcome! You're best bet is always to approach your partner when they are rested, calm, and not going through a difficult time.

- **Resist saying "but..." to soften the blow**

We always think we're doing someone a favor by starting with a positive before getting to the negative – but this is actually not true. Take, for example, the statement: "I love how passionate you've become about home-decorating and I think you've got some great ideas, but I'm just not sure I like these new changes."

As soon as the "but" comes into play, the earlier part of the sentence doesn't mean anything. It can be even more upsetting because you've gotten your partner's hopes up by starting with something so positive, but these hopes are completely trampled on by the time you finish the sentence. Your partner is smart! They know the real point is everything that comes after the "but." Don't try to soften the blow with this (bad) technique, and instead do it through careful language. Speaking of which...

- **Utilize all you've learned about gentle and constructive language**

We brought up constructive language in an earlier chapter, and it's time to put that lesson to good use. This is the perfect time to use your "I" or "I feel" statements! Instead of voicing your concerns in terms of what your partner did, reframe them so it's about what you feel. Steer clear of absolute language and assumptions, and ensure no sentence starts with "you."

If you're upset about how they rarely help with chores, resist the urge to say, "You never help with chores and you don't care about how it affects me." Instead, try saying something like, "I feel like I'm not getting enough help with chores. I'd feel a lot better if we could have a more even distribution of tasks." Notice that there is no mention of "you" at all. This is ideal because your partner doesn't feel cornered and it doesn't make any assumptions. We are also reducing the chance of an argument because it's difficult to argue with how someone feels. That's their reality.

- **Prepare for pushback or questions**

You should always prepare for the possibility of your partner pushing back a little. This doesn't necessarily mean it'll be with anger or frustration, but if you think there's a chance it might happen, then definitely prepare for it. Consider all the ways your partner might try to argue with it and think of a constructive, confident answer. This is especially important if you're the more submissive partner and you have a tendency to give in. For example, the second partner in the previous scenario might say, "But I washed the dishes last week" or "But I'm not as good at doing chores as you." You know your partner well enough to anticipate with some accuracy what their protests might be. Even if their responses are infuriating, stay calm and constructive.

- **Conclude with solutions and positivity**

Don't just sit and stew in the problem at hand, be ready to come up with a solution. Your partner may have some ideas as well, but for the best outcome, bring your own ideas to the table. Think of the next step and give your partner a place to start. This is the best way to work through a concern because you're essentially saying "This problem is easy to solve and here, this is the perfect opportunity. We can start making things better right now!"

Going back to our example problem, the concerned partner could then say, "I think a great way to resolve this would be to take turns each week doing the chores. How about I do the rest of this week and you can start on Monday?" Notice how this makes the situation instantly seem more positive. The problem is not the point anymore, it's the solution.

As we mentioned in a previous point, it's not a good idea to start the discussion with a "but" statement where you go from positive to negative – but the reverse is a much better idea. Add the positive statement to the end of the conversation so it can end on a good note.

## 5 Statements to Instantly Defuse a Heated Discussion

It happens in every relationship. Sometimes you find yourself in a talk with your partner that's gone from perfectly chill to blazing hot – and not in a good way. Perhaps it's because they've just had a hard day and they're in a bad mood, or perhaps they just woke up on the wrong side of the bed. Whatever it is, you can't seem to tame the fire in their attitude and all you know is it needs to stop now. Keep these statements in your back pocket to immediately calm a heated situation:

1. **"I see your point."**

When we say this, we validate our partner's point of view. This can calm someone down because all we really want is to make our point understood. We continue arguing because we want to make ourselves heard. Eliminate the need to continue arguing, by saying they have already made themselves heard.

## 2. "I understand."

This statement is ideal for defusing a situation without giving in. By saying you understand you are not admitting you are wrong; you are just saying you comprehend their view. Similar to the previous statement, you are letting them know what they've said has been thoughtfully received.

## 3. "What can I do to make it better?"

Instead of fueling the argument, try shifting the conversation to possible solutions. Without stirring the pot, you're letting your partner know you're ready to fix the situation. This will make them more willing to cooperate. This statement works wonders, but you must be willing to put in extra work. Since you are letting your partner know you want to make things better, you need to follow up on that promise.

## 4. "What do you need right now?"

Like the previous response, you're skipping the argument and going straight to the solution. Your partner will be more touched by this question because you're asking them directly what they need. This can cut to the core of an argument because you're saying, "I know it's not really about this. I know it's about you, and what you're not getting. I want to take care of that." Take on a more nurturing attitude and be willing to do what your partner says they need.

5. **"I'm sorry."**

Don't underestimate the power of apologies. It can whittle a fiery blaze down to a single burning ember. Sometimes, it's just not worth arguing till our heads turn blue. Apologizing is not always about admitting defeat or letting your partner win, it's about choosing harmony over your ego. It doesn't always mean "You're right, I'm wrong" sometimes it can mean "It hurts me to see you so upset and I'm sorry you feel this way."

## What NOT to Say During an Argument

We've covered what you should say. Now, let's get to what you definitely shouldn't say. If you're in a heated discussion or an argument, steer clear of the following phrases and sentences if you want to prevent an explosion.

1. **"Calm down."**

It's a big claim, but I'll say it: never in the history of mankind has an urge to "calm down" actually calmed an upset person down. Even if you mean well, this comes off as condescending and unsympathetic. The person who needs to calm down is actually in deep need of empathy and understanding; this statement demonstrates the opposite of that. It shows that the non-upset person doesn't understand at all, since they think it should be so easy for their partner to stop expressing their emotions in that moment. If you say this, you will not get a positive response. Avoid it at all costs and instead try asking them to share more with you.

2. **"Not this again!"**

If your partner is upset and you bemoan the fact they're upset about something *again*, this will only create more anger. By saying this, we're invalidating our partner. We're showing annoyance and impatience at their true feelings. We're essentially saying we don't care because they've been upset about it before. Instead of showing care, we are being condescending and implying their reaction is ridiculous.

3. **"If you don't ____ then I'm breaking up with you."**

This is a big no-no in relationships. In fact, many people consider it emotional abuse. If you're threatening your partner with a break-up in order to get them to do something, you're displaying cruel behavior, especially if you're not really serious. Even if you are, however, phrasing it as a threat could still cause a lot of damage. If your partner stops whatever they're doing and you continue to be in a relationship, this moment will leave them with a lot of anxiety. They will begin to feel as if they're walking on eggshells. If they start to make changes for you, they will only be acting out of fear, instead of love.

To properly convey how you feel without resorting to threats, remember to use "I" statements. Instead of saying, "If you don't stop talking to him, I'm breaking up with you" try saying, "I feel very upset by how much you talk to this other guy. It's starting to bother me on a deep level and I worry it's affecting my ability to be a healthy partner for you."

# 9 Relationship Problems You Cannot Fix

Try as hard as you may, there are some issues in a relationship that cannot be helped nine out of ten times. You may be a master communicator, and perhaps even your partner as well, but sometimes, there's only so much you can do. If your relationship has any of the following problems, it may be best to walk away before both partners begin to hurt.

1. **Serial cheating**

One instance of infidelity can really tear a relationship to shreds, but even then, it's salvageable – if the cheating partner makes lasting changes to their behavior. But continuous infidelity is a different issue. This indicates the cheating partner has a real problem, and they can't be in a healthy relationship until they solve it on their own. Stop making allowances for a partner that constantly cheats on you. It will only lead to more pain. No amount of good communication will fix this. It is entirely up to the cheating partner to do the self-work. And if they haven't started now, why wait around and continue to get hurt?

### 2. Too much contempt

It's normal to be mad at your partner for something, but contempt is a different story. Contempt runs deeper and is far more persistent. It happens when one partner can't let something go. It's begun to gnaw at them, they can't forget it or forgive, and it's caused resentment to build. The fault could be anyone's. It could be the non-contemptuous partner's fault for deeply hurting his or her partner, or it could be the contemptuous partner's fault for refusing to heal and let go. A little scorn is normal after an upsetting event, but it transforms into contempt when time has passed, and time has healed no wounds whatsoever.

### 3. Narcissistic personality disorder

There's a big difference between being a narcissist and being a clinical Narcissist, i.e. having Narcissistic Personality Disorder. If your partner is a little vain, occasionally makes big-headed statements, but can still take accountability for his mistakes, then your partner is likely just a regular lowercase narcissist. They may be annoying sometimes, but they don't have a personality disorder, and you can still make progress with them. A Narcissist, on the other hand, cannot be fixed and it's best to step away now before you get more hurt. Clinical Narcissists are unable to take accountability for anything and they have an unwillingness to recognize the needs of other people. It is not possible for them to be in a healthy, happy relationship.

## 4. Conflicting goals

You may have all the same common interests, but at the end of the day, conflicting goals can be a killer. Some partners may be lucky enough to settle on a compromise, but some goals are on opposite ends of the spectrum. If you desperately want kids and your partner doesn't want them at all, there's no way to compromise on this. Unless someone changes their mind, both partners cannot get what they want and this means one partner is doomed to feel unsatisfied. This can lead to resentment and may even ruin a connection. In the end, it can result not only in pain, but a lot of wasted time.

## 5. Abuse

If one partner engages in abusive behavior, whether physical or emotional, the relationship should end as soon as possible. Abusive behavior is toxic and will only drag both partners into a cycle of pain that continues on until it's off-the-charts. The abusive partner is always at fault and their behavior demonstrates they are incapable of being in a healthy relationship at the current stage in their life. It is advised that this partner leaves the relationship, stops hurting the other partner, and pursues therapy so they evolve into more healthy, loving companion.

The abusive partner is less likely to admit what they're doing is a problem, so it may be up to the abused partner to find the strength to leave. Friends and family are in the best position to end such a volatile relationship. If you are close to someone who is suffering from abuse, see if you can assist in getting them out of the bad situation.

### 6. Failure to grow

Conflict is a natural part of any relationship, and if both partners are healthy, they should be finding ways to achieve better harmony. For one reason or another, however, one or both partners may find there's a persistent lack of growth. In other words, there's a quality or behavior pattern that has continued to have a negative effect without any improvement, even though our partner knows we want to see change. This is only a big problem if the behavior that needs to be grown out of is affecting the happiness of the relationship.

For example, if your partner has been working on his anger issues for years but is still as turbulent as he was in the beginning, reconsider whether you can put up with this for the future to come. If your partner continues to flirt with other people even though you've repeatedly pointed out it bothers you, it's likely this will not ever change. At a certain point, it becomes clear when certain issues are here to stay and it's important that we make the right decision concerning our future. Either this behavior is too deeply ingrained in their personalities or they aren't motivated to seek out this growth. Choose what's right for your sanity and stop waiting for change that likely won't come.

### 7. Constant and pointless arguing

We may go through periods of bickering with our partners – especially if we're going through a rough patch in our lives – but if this occurrence is persistent and a constant drain on your energy, it's time to stop and think. Frequent pointless arguing is often a sign of a much deeper problem. Sometimes both partners have stopped being compatible, fallen out of love, or have developed deep resentment for each other. It's very rare that these problems can be fixed. If it has become easier to be apart from your partner than be with them, it may be time to put a cork in it.

### 8. Inability to trust

It's true what they say; without trust, a relationship is nothing. Trust forms the foundation of every relationship. And without a strong foundation, it doesn't matter how glamorous and impressive the rest of it is, it'll come crumbling down as soon as the wind changes. Once trust is broken, it's extremely difficult to rebuild. It can take years and a lot of hard work if a couple decides to try and make it work, and even then, sometimes it is not successful. In every relationship, we should have the basic assurance that our partner won't hurt or betray us. Consider how deeply broken the trust is and whether you ever see yourself fully recovering.

## 9. Deep feelings for a third party

We can all get over lust or a mild crush, but if it's more than that, we're dealing with something else entirely. Sometimes, the feelings one partner has for a third party are very deep, and they may even be verging on love. For feelings to get to this point, the partner in question would have to be exposed to this third party for an extended period of time. We know this because it takes a while for deep feelings to develop.

There's a lot less hope for the relationship if the partner in question has been intentionally seeking out the company of this third party. This behavior displays a big problem with self-control – and this could pose a serious problem to the relationship down the road. If this scenario takes place, it may be beneficial for the relationship to end.

It's a slightly different story if the partner with feelings has developed them due to involuntary exposure, for example, through work. In this case, it is not a self-control issue and there is hope. The only way to fix it, however, is by completely removing oneself from all situations involving the third party. If this is a co-worker, it means making a big decision, such as quitting the job causing exposure. Otherwise, these feelings will only grow.

## Relationship Communication

The good news is that the majority of partners can, indeed, work through their problems. If your relationship issue wasn't listed, there are higher chances for you working out your issues. And while the problems listed are mostly unfixable, there will always be exceptions. In any case, it always takes a lot of hard work, kind communication, and incredible cooperation to see positive change.

# Chapter Eight - Deepening the Bond

There's always more we can do to deepen the bond in our relationship. At the end of the day, we shouldn't just feel like lovers; we should also feel like friends and to an extent, family. When we feel a strong connection to our partners, there is a much higher likelihood that communication will be kind, helpful, and transformative. And in addition to this, a good connection means we're much more likely to follow up on our compromises and be a better partner. When we feel close to someone, we instantly feel more compassionate and empathetic. These two qualities are necessary for a loving connection.

As excellent as these bonding techniques may be, they require commitment from both partners to be completely effective. A positive outcome takes effort and attention; it does not simply fall into your lap after one attempt. Keep these activities and exercises in mind for the rest of your future to come. Even when relationship communication is good, this is no reason to stop seeking out opportunities to bond.

## Exercises and Activities that Strengthen Relationships

- **Start a love journal with your partner**

This practice does wonders for maintaining romantic connections. Start off by purchasing a journal (ideally together) that you both love the look of. If you don't live together, then aim to take turns with the journal. Come up with a schedule that works for you. Will the journal pass hands weekly? Fortnightly? Whenever you feel like it? Whatever works for you!

If you do live together, keep the journal in a private area of the house, but one where you frequently pass by. Again, the arrangement of who and when to write is up to you. I advise writing something every day, even if it's very short, or taking turns. If you decide to take turns, find a creative way to indicate who the last writer was, without opening the book. This will ensure you aren't constantly checking it to see if it's been updated.

What's great about this activity is that you can make the rules. Will the book be filled with love letters? Will it all be written in haikus? If one partner is upset, should they write an honest, open letter about how they feel in the journal? Or will this only be reserved for romance? It's totally up to you.

- **Role reversal**

This exercise is great for when two people are trying to see eye-to-eye on a problem. For this exercise to succeed, you and your partner should both be calm and willing to fully cooperate. If there's a hint of snark or sarcasm, abandon the attempt and try again during a better mood.

In this role reversal exercise, you and your partner will have a conversation about a problem at hand, but you'll both speak from the other person's point-of-view. Each of you should really think about what the other partner would say and consider real reasons they might use. One of the reasons this exercise is so effective is because it eliminates the need to "win" the discussion. Partners are forced to think deeply about their loved one's perspective, and this instantly helps couples empathize with each other.

- **The eye contact exercise**

For this exercise, you and your partner should sit across from each other. Ideally, lights should be dim and you should be close to each other, but not too close. Wherever you choose to sit, make sure it's comfortable. It's also important there's no talking or touching during this exercise.

## Relationship Communication

Set a timer for five minutes and aim to look into each others' eyes for the full length of those five minutes. Eye contact should be gentle and uninterrupted. Do not stare intensely at your partner and always remember to blink as you would normally.

You might be surprised by how fast five minutes goes by. Couples can get so lost that they actually lose track of time. After this exercise, you'll feel a heightened sense of connection and attunement with your partner. If a distance has grown between the two of you, this exercise can help bring you back to the same wavelength.

- **Create a vision board**

Get creative with your partner and work on a vision board together. A vision board is a motivational collage of photos, notes, and anything that gets across the future you'd most like to have together. This can include places you'd like to travel to or photos of your dream house together. Whatever fills you both with hope, joy, and positivity about what's to come. It's important that both partners contribute something to this vision board. Remember that it's your *shared* vision, not just one partner's fantasy. And most of all, have fun with it. This is an incredibly fun way to strengthen your connection with your partner. You don't need an artistic streak to enjoy it!

- **Go through the famous '36 Questions that Lead to Love'**

In a famous experiment conducted by psychologists, a significant number of people felt a stronger connection after going through a series of questions together. Many of them even claimed to have fallen in love. Ultimately, the experiment proves that when both partners are engaging in personal self-disclosure, acting vulnerably, and actively listening to their partner, an immediate connection is formed. By forcing two people to do just this, a sense of closeness and intimacy was fostered. Although this experiment was conducted

## Relationship Communication

on people who didn't know each other, existing couples still benefit greatly from this bonding exercise.

The 36 questions are separated into three sets, which each one becoming more personal than the last. Take turns answering these questions:

### **Set 1**

1. Whom would you invite to be your dinner guest, given the choice of absolutely anyone in the world?
2. Would you like to be famous? If so, in what way?
3. Before making a phone call, do you rehearse what you're going to say? If so, why do you do this?
4. What constitutes a perfect day in your eyes?
5. When was the last time you sang to yourself? And when was the last time you sang for someone else?
6. If you lived to the age of 90 and had the choice of either the body or mind of a 30-year old for the last 60-years of your life, which would you choose?
7. Do you have any idea how you might die?
8. List three things that you and your partner seem to have in common.
9. What are you most grateful for about your life?
10. If you could change anything at all about the way you were raised, what would you change?
11. Share your life story in as much detail as possible but take only 4 minutes and no longer.
12. If you could acquire any quality or ability overnight, what would you choose?

## Relationship Communication

### Set 2

13. If you came upon a crystal ball that could tell you any truth about your life, yourself, your future, or anything else, what would you most want to know?

14. Is there anything that you've dreamed of doing for a long time but haven't ever done? Why haven't you done it yet?

15. What would you say is the greatest accomplishment of your life?

16. What are the qualities and behaviors you most value in a friendship?

17. Talk about your most treasured memory.

18. Now talk about your worst memory.

19. If you knew that you'd die suddenly in a year, is there anything you'd change about the way you're living now? What would that be and why?

20. Describe what friendship means to you.

21. How important are love and affection to you? What roles do they play in your life?

22. Take turns sharing a positive characteristic about each other. Each partner should share five things for a total of ten.

23. How close is your family? Are you warm towards each other? Do you think your childhood was happier than the average childhood?

24. What's your relationship with your mother like? How do you feel about it?

### Set 3

25. Take turns sharing three statements, each one beginning with "we." For example, "we're in this room feeling…"

26. Finish this sentence: "I wish I had someone with whom I could share…"

27. If you and your partner were to become close friends, what would be important for them to know?

28. Tell your partner what you honestly like them. This time, try and share something you wouldn't normally say to someone you'd just met.

29. Talk about one of the most embarrassing moments of your life.

30. When was the last time you cried in front of another person? When was the last time you cried by yourself?

31. Share something that you like about your partner already.

32. In your opinion, what is too serious to be joked about, if anything?

33. If you were to die tonight without the opportunity to communicate with anyone, what would you most regret not having told someone? Why haven't you told them yet?

34. Your house, containing everything you own, catches fire. You've saved your loved ones and pets, and now you only have time to save one more item. What would you save? Why?

35. Of all the people in your family, whose death upset and disturb you the most? Why?

36. Share a personal problem with your partner and ask for their advice on how they might handle it. After this, the partner who offered advice should reflect how the asker seems to be feeling about the chosen problem.

# Bond Instantly with these 8 Fun Couple Activities

When it comes down to it, the secret to nurturing your bond is stepping outside of your comfort zone and giving your partner your full attention. Feel free to seek that out in any way you choose, but I highly advise starting with these highly effective methods well known for strengthening bonds instantly.

### 1. Massaging each other

This highly sensual act does more than heat things up, it also asks each partner to engage in a few moments of total kindness towards their loved one. For the length of each massage, one partner is giving completely to their partner without getting anything in return. They are focused on their partner's pleasure entirely and concerned only with creating an enjoyable experience for them through the power of touch. People are so accustomed to physical intimacy and touch strictly being part of sex that it can be wildly exciting to have both those things without sexual contact. This closeness through non-sexual touch is what creates the bond. For the best outcome, both partners should take turns and each massage should take the same length of time.

### 2. Go out dancing

Dancing is about as close as you can get to sexual intercourse without actually having it! For that reason, dancing can be a real fire-starter in a relationship; not just in the passion department, but even in terms of our connection. It doesn't matter what language you speak or what culture you're from, dancing has a knack for inducing joy and releasing tension in the body. When we do this with our partner, we're expressing ourselves without saying a word. The act of moving in alignment and in rhythm with each other is its own collaborative exercise, and it can be a wonderful symbol for loving each other in harmony. If you and your partner are on the shier side, why not have a drink or two to open you up?

### 3. Work out together

Believe it or not, numerous studies have proven that working out with your partner boosts overall happiness in your relationship. Researchers have found that this is particularly true for exercises that require both partners to get up and move together in some fashion. Bonding happens at a subconscious level when we engage in the mirror effect. This is the neurological process that leads to bonding and manifests as mirrored movements. By coordinating our actions or mirroring each other's movements, we are firing off mirror neurons and subsequently, deepening our bond.

And that's not all! Studies have also found that working out with a partner leads to improved workout performances. When someone is watching, we are more likely to push harder to try and avoid looking weak. Bond harder and get hotter: doesn't that sound like a great idea?

### 4. Go on a fancy date

The reason fancy dates have such a positive effect is simple: it gets us out of our routine and forces us to make ourselves look good for our partner. It's no secret that when we take care of ourselves and our appearance, our partner will find us more attractive. Couple this with an exciting scenario you don't normally experience and *voila,* you've started to reboot your connection. If your relationship has started to feel too comfortable, then consider taking your partner out to a nice restaurant. The formality of a fancy date offers a refreshing change from lounging around in sweatpants and it can instantly spice up a boring relationship.

## Relationship Communication

### 5. Visit the location of one of your "firsts"

Every couple has a unique love story. Even if it wasn't love at first sight or you had an unconventional start, it can be nice to take a walk down memory lane every once in a while. Why not visit the place where you met or where you had your first kiss? Retracing our steps can remind us of how far we've come with our significant other. If you do this with your partner, you'll relive the rush and the butterflies for just a moment; places attached to strong memories inevitably send us back in time. Enjoy these memories with each other and savor the beauty of your one-of-a-kind story, even if it wasn't perfect. Remember that at one point in time, where you are now was where you hoped to be.

### 6. Go on a trip together

A study conducted by the U.S. Travel Association found that couples who travel together are a great deal more satisfied in their relationships than those who don't. Still, many couples are hesitant to go on a trip because they're convinced that doing this will drain their bank account. This isn't true at all.

To experience the benefits of travel, all couples need to do is to get out of their comfort zone (not just psychologically but geographically as well!) and see something new and exciting. If you've got the budget for it, then sure, visit Paris or Rome, but you can have just as much fun going on a road trip to the next state over. Visit a National Park and stay at a 2 or 3-star hotel, or a humble inn. Get out into nature. Do something you don't normally do. This change of scenery can provide a much needed break from your rigid routine and you'll find your bond deepening naturally as you experience the wider world together.

### 7. Visit an amusement park

Kid or not, let's face it, amusement parks are incredibly fun. If you don't have a crippling fear of heights, take a break from your routine and spend a day at one with your significant other. Your relationship will see a number of benefits. For starters, thrilling rides will give you a rush of endorphins, meaning you'll feel overcome with happy feelings and a natural high. You'll also be pumped through with adrenaline, a neurotransmitter which is known to create memories in the mind. This means the wonderful day you've had will be solidified in your mind as a happy memory. Since you and your partner are encountering anxiety-inducing situations, you'll bond as you both seek out comfort and warmth in each other.

## 8. Cook together

If you're on a budget, cooking together is a great way to deepen the bond while also filling the belly. Cooking requires both partners to cooperate and work towards a common goal – exactly what being in a successful relationship is all about! This is great practice for getting in the right mindset for problem-solving and teamwork. Each partner is making their own contribution and the process challenges both partners to get on the same page, or the entire meal suffers.

A cooking project teaches us skills we need to bring into the rest of our relationship. And on top of this, we bond because we're creating something together. We're combining efforts for a tangible finished product. If we succeed in making a delicious meal, couples can bond over the shared pride. They'll likely feel like they can do anything as a team. But those who don't succeed, should not feel discouraged. This is not a reflection on your relationship; you may just need some more cooking practice!

Scroll through cooking websites or recipe books and decide on a meal that you'd like to recreate. This should be something you both love. If you're not experienced cooks, choose a dish with simple-

## Relationship Communication

enough instructions that you understand and make sure you possess all the necessary equipment.

Even the closest couples need to take time out to deepen their bond. It doesn't mean it's not already deep, it's about reaching out and reconnecting to remind yourselves why you're there. Time and routine can wear us down; seek out moments of intimacy to strengthen your bond. When we act from a place of deep bonding, relationship communication is more likely to be loving and effective.

Keep an open heart and be brave enough to leave your comfort zone so as to meet each other's need for adventure and variety. Instead of feeling mindless panic in an uncertain scenario, try and transform that feeling into the desire to problem-solve with your partner. Approach life with the mindset that you can do anything if you put your heads together, and you can solve any need you have, if you put your hearts together.

# Conclusion

Congratulations on making it to the end of *Relationship Communication*! Whether you realize it or not, you've made one giant leap in the right direction. This isn't just fantastic for you, but for your significant other. You'll both see benefits that impact your day-to-day habits and with continued practice of these techniques, the days of strained communication will feel long gone. By completing this book, you've demonstrated your commitment to more effective and loving communication – and this is one of the best things you could possibly do for the person you love. You're on the right track towards a stronger relationship. You should be proud of yourself!

While you've made a big first step, it's essential that you don't quit now. Relationship communication is an ongoing journey; you've been granted the tools and techniques, but now it's time to use them in real situations, in the real world. Don't make this a short-lived attempt, but incorporate these transformative practices into your daily life and make them last. Reinvent your norms entirely and create exemplary habits.

Make sure you understand the five vital needs that your relationship must fulfill for both partners to be happy. Perhaps work with your partner on identifying which of your needs have been fully met and which ones still remain unmet. This is an essential step to make before finding a solution. Once you've done this, assess your situation and see if you can figure out which stage your relationship is in. This will help you better understand what you're going through, and equally as helpful, it'll show you what else is to come.

I sure hope you were honest with yourself in the second chapter. Don't feel ashamed to admit your relationship has a problem. After all, we *must* do this before we can start making positive changes. Hopefully, you identified the reason why communication has been less than great and you've finally been made aware of any mistakes

## Relationship Communication

you're currently making. But of course, don't just dwell on these problems. As I mentioned, you need to start creating better habits. You've learned all about the habits that save relationships. Start using these right away!

You've delved deeper into the many ways we can express and receive love. Once you've worked out what your partner's love language is, try and think of creative ways to show them how much you care. In fact, I highly recommend going over the section with them so you, too, can let your love language be known. When couples have a good understanding of each other's love languages, a lot less becomes lost in translation. Suddenly both partners are on the same page. Without all the confusion of trying to understand each other, they can just focus on the exchange of love.

While habits are certainly helpful, the two people at the core of the relationship must be healthy halves of the whole to really make it work. In order to form a great partnership and be a good partner, it's necessary that we learn to be emotionally healthy individuals. We don't become perfect once we enter into a relationship; all the emotional baggage and trauma we experienced beforehand comes with us! If we're not careful, past hurts can seep into our communication habits and tinge them with negativity. With the new tools you've been provided with, you can focus all your energy on becoming a better partner. You can finally start putting the past behind you. Try and help your partner do the same. At the end of the day, make sure you're meeting each others' needs – not just the five basic ones, but also the unique needs that come with their personalities.

Treat every sensitive situation with care. Know when you are dealing with a ticking time-bomb, and refer back to the relevant chapter for the techniques you need during the hard conversations. By following this guide closely, you'll ensure that even through the harsh storms, you always stay afloat. There is no such thing as completely smooth

## Relationship Communication

sailing in a relationship, but you can survive and make the most of the journey with these important tools. When we handle these situations the right way, they become opportunities for deeper intimacy. They become open doors instead of walls and dead-ends.

Relationship communication doesn't come naturally to anyone; it always takes work, commitment, and incredible self-discipline. It is a choice that loving partners make for each other everyday, and those that make the effort, reap rewards that others can scarcely imagine. Stay self-aware and do what you can to deepen your bond. Even people who are exceptionally close need to find time to maintain their connection. Let the love you foster through these lessons power every interaction from now on. I've shown you the wonderful path ahead, now it's your turn to walk it together.

www.ingramcontent.com/pod-product-compliance
Lightning Source LLC
Chambersburg PA
CBHW030109100526
44591CB00009B/344